Praise for *Consider the Birds*

"A different kind of field guide! From the raven to the dove and the ostrich to the sparrow, Debbie Blue reminds us how rich the biblical account of the natural world can be, an endless source of metaphor and inspiration!"
—**Bill Mckibben**, founder of http://350.org

"Debbie Blue is simply one of my favorite preachers and writers in America today. *Consider the Birds* is a singular work of devotion and beauty that will make you fall in love with that which you may have never bothered to notice before. I cannot recommend it highly enough."
—**Rev. Nadia Bolz-Weber**, author of *Pastrix: The Cranky, Beautiful Faith of a Sinner & Saint*

"Debbie Blue points to the sky and the trees and the grimy sidewalks of our world the way she points to the Word, saying: "Wisdom: attend!" And through the birds and their Creator and our stories about both, Debbie Blue does midrash on their lives, revealing mysteries and heartbreak, pratfalls and glory. This is a brilliant, astonishing work of scholarship and attention that will become a classic of Christian writing."
—**Sara Miles**, author of *Take This Bread, Jesus Freak,* and *City of God*

"I would read Debbie Blue's grocery list. That's how much I love her writing. So, yes, I want to read her writings on birds—in the world and the Bible—about how birds are the 'currency of mercy,' about eating quail until it comes out of your nostrils, about the killing prowess of eagles. This is a book to be savored, to be read while sitting next to a lake, to be read aloud to a loved one, to be shelved with the most beautiful books you've ever read."
—**Tony Jones** (http://tonyj.net), theologian-in-residence at Solomon's Porch, Minneapolis, author, blogger

"Debbie Blue has a knack for noticing things, things of God and things of life. She not only notices, she sees. She sees the way spiritual guides see: with insight, clarity, wit, and truth. Debbie is at her best in *Consider the Birds,* and for those who are up for going on a journey of seeing the ways of the birds and of God, this book is a gem."
—**Doug Pagitt**, pastor, author, Goodness Conspirator

"Debbie Blue knows a lot about birds. She's ransacked history and mythology, not to mention her own backyard, for a wildly entertaining trove of obscure, comical, and sometimes downright revolting bits of lore about vultures, roosters, sparrows, and pigeons that we hardly notice when we're reading the Bible. But it's what Debbie knows about our hearts, and about the texture of life in our world today, and about God, that makes this book a real treasure. Debbie has a keen eye for the inhumane, the self-destructive, and the really stupid stuff that masquerades as cultural wisdom, conventional religion, and common sense, and the way she laughs at herself, and us too, when we unthinkingly fall into line is a big part of the charm of this book. In Debbie's sure hands, the Bible becomes a sly and paradoxical—and often very funny—collection of stories that doesn't say anywhere close to what we have been taught to think it says, and God becomes a presence so unrelentingly good that we can hardly believe it."
—**Doug Frank**, author of *A Gentler God*

"Why do Jesus and Debbie Blue both tell us to 'consider the birds'? Perhaps because a 'corporate person' has never seen a bird and never will. And perhaps because the visitations of spirit are very like being stunned by a wild bird and nothing like staring at a screen. Birds neither reap, sow, Tweet, nor Friend. They just fly into our lives with a powerless power rooted in the fact that beauty is truth and (as this delightful book and birdsong and Origen all agree) 'the fowls of the air are also within thee.' To see or hear a bird clearly, for the duration of that clarity, is to be the Way."
—**David James Duncan**, author of *The Brothers K* and *The River Why*

"Baby pelicans faint after feeding? A vulture collided with an airplane at 37,900 feet? How much there is to learn about birds! And, by following Debbie Blue's meditations on them, how much there is to learn from birds about the Creator and our place in Creation. This book is a delight."
—**Marilyn Nelson**, author of *Carver: A Life in Poems, A Wreath for Emmett Till,* and *Faster Than Light: New and Selected Poems*

"Blue's book is buoyant. We fly up like birds in a conversation about a supreme being—and I appreciated so the flight of this god-talk, a subject that doesn't usually fly anymore, encrusted as it is by gold, shadows, centuries…"
—**Rev. Billy Talen**, founder of the Church of Stop Shopping, author of *The End of the World*

CONSIDER
the
BIRDS

DEBBIE BLUE

A PROVOCATIVE
GUIDE TO
BIRDS *of the* BIBLE

ABINGDON PRESS
Nashville

CONSIDER THE BIRDS
A PROVOCATIVE GUIDE TO THE BIRDS OF THE BIBLE

Copyright © 2013 by Debbie Blue

Library of Congress Cataloging-in-Publication Data

Blue, Debbie.
    Consider the birds : a provocative guide to the birds of the bible / Debbie Blue.
    1 online resource.
    Description based on print version record and CIP data provided by publisher; resource not viewed.
    ISBN 978-1-4267-4950-6 (epub)—ISBN 978-1-4267-4950-6 (binding: soft black / paper / with flaps : alk. paper)   1. Birds in the Bible,   I. Title.
    BS664
    220.8'598—dc23
                                                                          2013014556

Illustrations by Jim Larson.

13 14 15 16 17 18 19 20 21 22—10 9 8 7 6 5 4 3 2 1
MANUFACTURED IN THE UNITED STATES OF AMERICA

CONTENTS

FOREWORD

by Lauren Winner

Debbie Blue's book is the best I've read all year. I say that despite the fact that I cannot tell a warbler from a wren, cannot remember if cardinals are harbingers of winter or spring, and, indeed, am really not interested in birds at all. (Maybe this is because I have damaged hearing and can't hear high-pitched noises—would I care about birds more if I could hear their cheeps and chirps?)

I am, however, interested in the Bible.

If you're like me, you think that one of the amazing things about the Bible is that it seems so multilayered—there seems always to be another layer of meaning. Even when I think I "understand" a biblical story, even when I think I've gotten to "the" kernel of insight the story holds—it turns out there is something more there, something I haven't seen yet. As a rabbi with the alliterative name Ben Bag Bag once said of the Jewish Scriptures, "Turn it and turn it, for everything is in it. Look deeply into it, and grow old with it, and spend time over it, and do not stir from it, because there is no greater portion." Turn it and turn it—there is always more to see.

That amazes me. That is why the Bible is different from *Pride and Prejudice* or *Little Women*. There is *a lot* to see in

Pride and Prejudice and *Little Women*. There is much to see. But I do not for a minute believe that even the best novel is somehow endlessly overflowing with meaning in the same way that the Bible is. This amazes me, this endless overflowing of the Bible.

**

It also amazes me that those endless layers of meaning are so hard to see, so difficult to discern.

I am amazed by the number of times I sit down with a passage of Scripture and feel that it says nothing at all. That it is mute. That it is boring. Or that it says one thing, and I already saw the one thing nine years ago, and here the passage is still saying that one thing. Ho-hum.

Maybe you're different, but I need guides when it comes to Scripture. I need teachers and readers and friends who see things in Scripture that I do not see, who can show me those layers of meaning when all I see is ho-hum.

In my experience, there is no better guide to the Bible than Debbie Blue. I could listen to her talk about the Bible all week. And I would see something I hadn't seen before every hour of that week. Truly, if I could read, forever and ever, only one person's illumination of the Bible—if I could have one person, and interpretations or sermons or insights by no other people—I'd pick Debbie Blue. (It's nice, of course, that I don't have to make that choice. If you like Debbie Blue's readings, you might also like the ways the Bible is read and interpreted by Ellen Davis and Avivah Gottlieb Zornberg and Bryna Jocheved Levy and Barbara Brown Taylor and Sarah Jobe.)

I could tell you how irreverent Debbie Blue is. I could tell you that though irreverent, she is also deeply reverent. I could tell you about her quirky perspective, and her even quirkier voice; I could tell you how much you will just downright enjoy passing the hours with this book. All of that is true, but what I really want to tell you is something less frothy than irreverence and quirk. I want to tell you that you will be deeply nourished and edified by this book.

Edified is an old-fashioned word; it comes from a Latin term meaning "to instruct or improve spiritually." Yes, this is a book that surprises and entertains. It is also—more importantly, more seriously—a book that will improve you spiritually.

In *Consider the Birds,* you will learn about not just birds. You willlearn about sacrifice, and salvation, and desire. Along the way you will also learn a little about Ishtar, and about masculinity. And you will learn something about quail and pigeons. (I promise, pigeons are more interesting than you realize.) What you will learn most about, though, is God. Who knew that biblical birds held so many of the keys to what the Scriptures have to say about God? Yet birds do. You will learn about God, and you will learn something about yourself—about how God sees you, and how you might more wholly dwell with this God who is sometimes imaged as a pigeon or a hen.

And when you go back to the Bible, you might, if you are lucky, periodically hear Debbie's voice in your head, inviting you to look for those layers of meaning in places you wouldn't have thought to look before. After I read *Consider the Birds,* I found myself noticing, in a way I previously had not, various flowers in the Bible. *What really is a rose of Sharon?* I wondered as I was reading the Song of Songs. *And what might it have to show me about God, or about myself?* In other words, Debbie Blue does the best kind of teaching—she shows us things we had not seen before, and she models how we might go and do likewise. So read here about the God who is revealed by birds, but do not be surprised if next time you are in the Scriptures, you find yourself thinking something wonderful about a lily or a cedar tree or a giant. Or an asp!

**

I will read this book again many times, I am sure, but I am envious that you are about to read it for the first time. You are in for a treat. You are in for delight, and for a new vision of birds and the Bible—and you are in for an encounter with God.

INTRODUCTION

 I DID NOT START paying attention to birds in earnest until I was twenty-five years old. I was dating a younger man at the time who was a naturalist. He took me birding in the arboretum at the University of Wisconsin, Madison. I was working in campus ministry at the time—he was a student. I didn't like getting up early, and I had a difficult time finding the birds in my binoculars. I'm not sure if I ever quite managed to focus on one, but his enthusiasm was boundless and I really liked him. He was two feet taller than me and he wrote beautiful poetry.

Not long after, I met a man of a more suitable age for me—who was also a birder. I fell in love with him in large part because he taught me to identify warblers. Falling in love and identifying birds have similar effects. Normal life is altered; every experience heightened; what was mundane begins to explode with meaning. You think birds are just birds—undifferentiated fluttering, then you find one magnified in your lens. You recognize its unique markings, lines, and color. Your heart pounds. It is a cerulean warbler. It is your new mate. I believe both things have equal power to change your life. I'm not kidding. Jim and I spent our courtship looking for birds. We drove to Nebraska to see the cranes do their mating dances. We bought a VW van and drove out west. We stopped the bus and got out our binoculars anytime we saw a duck in a puddle. We didn't care much about a wedding—we got married in a park in Seattle. We began to keep our life list, checking off birds.

For all that, I can't say I'm a birder. I quit keeping the list after Jim and I had kids; and although we have binoculars hanging from a beam in our house, I have not pursued birding with the same intensity I have given other things. I started a church, House of Mercy, with a couple of friends in St. Paul. We bought a farm an hour north of the city where we live with three other human families and the occasional threesome of sandhill cranes, a pair of nesting bald eagles, bird-killing cats, beautiful gardens, chickens, bunnies, and paths by the river.

I have never stopped admiring people who get up early in the morning to wait quietly for small colorful (or drab) gifts to appear in the bushes. I'm convinced that there is something about the sort of consciousness necessary for birding that is very much like the practice of faith. It comes and it goes. It requires waiting. You must use both your body and your mind. Attention is paramount. Whenever a bird showed up in a text I was preaching on, I would become (perhaps inordinately) intrigued by it. With some encouragement from an editor, I decided to write this book. I knew it would get me paying attention to birds again, make me pick up the binoculars. And I am always looking for new ways into the text of the Bible—I thought taking the birds seriously as characters (minor as they might be) might lead down some interesting and unusual paths. I think it has.

Birds are everywhere in the Bible, from start to finish. God hovers over the face of the water in Genesis—the ancient rabbis suggest—like a bird. Birds gorge on the flesh of the defeated "beast" in Revelation. They are the currency of mercy—the birds of sacrifice. They bring bread to the prophets. They are food for the wanderers. Abraham has to shoo them away from his offering, and a pigeon goes with Jesus on his first visit to the temple. God is a bird who carries the Israelites on her wings—a bird under whose feathers we will find refuge. Jesus compares himself to a hen. He tells us to "consider the birds." I love a guy who says that, obviously.

Birds have a prominent place in the Judeo-Christian founding narratives, as well as the founding narratives of almost every culture and religion. As long as humans have been breathing, they've been investing birds with meaning. They are not just bones and feathers—they are strength or hope, omen or oracle—the spirit has wings. Birds are in the legends of gods, the iconography of the church, and the lexicon of tattoo artists.

People identify with birds. We watch them, research them, tell stories about them, and in the process we explore our humanity and inhumanity—mystery and manners. They're funny and dirty, noble and shifty—much like us.

Once you start looking for birds, you will find them every-where—in your bushes, of course, but they are also in alleys and mines and caves. Every songwriter I've ever loved, almost every poet I know, has written words about birds. I pick up my *Harper's*, my *New Yorker*, even the *Nation*, and there are stories, essays, poems about birds. I have heard about three new bands in the last week: Sleeping in the Aviary, Birds and Batteries, and the Larks.

I believe it is the same way with the grace of God—when you start paying attention, you'll discover it in places you hadn't noticed it before. It may make your heart race, or help you breathe. It can free you from anxiety (at least now and again). My hope in writing this book was to get myself and readers deeply paying attention—to what flits by us on any given day, to the layers of meaning in sacred text.

Considering the birds is different than considering rocket science or technology; it gets you thinking different thoughts about creatures, creation, and the creator. Whatever bird I looked at and studied, however each was represented in the text, I was again and again struck by the vulnerability. Their flight is amazing; but it is because of their hollow bones, the fragile strength of their feathers, that they can fly. A bird can grow a new feather in two weeks—it can also be wiped out so easily. Many birds are on the brink of extinction. Without human influence (habitat destruction, climate change), the expected rate of extinction for birds would be around one species per century. Some reports say we are losing ten species a year. I hope considering the birds will motivate us to press for more responsible human behavior. If, as Emily Dickinson wrote, "hope is the thing with feathers," you'd think we'd be passionate about keeping it alive.

THE
PIGEON

PURITY
and IMPURITY

THE VERY FIRST STORY in the Bible includes birds. In Genesis 1, God says, "Let birds fly," and "Let the birds multiply." But even before God creates the birds, the spirit of God hovers over the face of the deep—the ancient rabbis suggest— like a bird. The Talmud even specifies what kind of bird—a dove: "The Spirit of God hovered over the surface of the waters—like a dove." Not a pterodactyl or the humongous forbidding birds found in many creation myths, but a gentle, quiet, friendly thing. It's surprising. Of course the rabbis might have been wrong about the attributes of the spirit of God at creation; a giant powerful bird is a more likely character to take on the void. What chance would a dove have with the deep and the dark? It has a small brain, stubby little legs—it is easy picking for predators.

It is not difficult information to uncover; nevertheless, I was surprised to find that a dove is, in fact, a pigeon by another name.

Pigeon is from the French *pijon,* and *dove* is an English word. There are a great variety of birds English speakers call either pigeons or doves—all in the Columbidae family. We tend to call the more delicate and smaller members of the family "doves," but the names are interchangeable. This information is hard to absorb. How could a pigeon command creation? The rabbis have wild imaginations. Still, I like the image quite a bit—the spirit of God—like a pigeon.

In the beginning of the Gospel of Luke, the spirit of God hovers over Mary. The Spirit hovered over the deep in Genesis and made it pregnant so that the deep birthed creation; now it hovers over Mary and makes her pregnant. Christian art through the centuries has depicted this hovering presence, in the spirit of the rabbis, as a dove. I hope to show that this image is both stranger and richer than we normally think.

Once we get to the baptism of Jesus, the text is explicit. Here the spirit of God shows up, and this time each of the Gospel writers is clear: LIKE A DOVE. The heavens open and the spirit of God comes down, alighting on Jesus' shoulder, and a voice from heaven says, "This is my Son . . . with whom I am well pleased." I have always thought that the voice seemed like a bit much: far-fetched, B movie-ish. And the dove here has never moved me. Maybe because it is such a familiar scene or because I've seen too many bad illustrations of it, or because the white dove has been overused as a symbol in commercial Christianity. It is shorthand for "purity and innocence." When the church we rent puts up doves at Pentecost, we take them down before we proceed with our worship. It doesn't have the right vibe. They seem trite and sentimental—Styrofoam birds and white felt cutout doves glued on a red background. What good news could they possibly bring?

John the Baptist says, "I saw the Spirit descend as a dove from heaven, and it remained on him." This, says John, is how he knows he should believe in Jesus. Somehow that has always seemed a little thin to me: something that happens in fairy tales, not something that could hold much weight. I have hardly stopped to consider the bird. I think, *Oh—it's a sign,* like something written on cardboard, or illuminated at the airport, or advertising a restaurant: Exit. Stop. Go. Eat here. This is the Messiah, flash flash. The Spirit descends like a dove, but I have often thought "like a dove" is extraneous information. It's the message, not the messenger, that's important here.

The dove is merely a conveyor of information, nothing more. And the message is flat—like black-and-white letters on a piece of paper. Something you could roll up and put into a small tube and attach to the bird's leg: *This is the messiah period believe in him period.* Homing doves have, in fact, been used precisely this way for thousands of years. Their unique (and still somewhat mysterious) homing ability means you can bring them with you, say, on a military campaign and then send them home bearing news of the battle. Or use them like the Greeks did, to inform the populace who the winners were at the Olympic games. You fold up a piece of papyrus and fit it in a tube and the bird will deliver it remarkably reliably. Is this all there is to the bird in this story?

PIGEON POST

Pigeons/doves have served every empire from the Egyptian to the Roman to the United States of America. They were used as spies in World Wars I and II. They were fitted with cameras, trained by soldiers, sent out in balloons. Although the white dove became the symbol for peace, many other pigeons are celebrated for their military service. The bird is not simply one thing. The most famous pigeon warrior was Cher Ami, who saved an American troop that was being fired on by both sides. He flew through enemy fire to deliver a message to the allied command that they were shooting at their own men. He was awarded the Croix de Guerre medal for his heroic flight. When he died he was stuffed. You can see him on display at the Smithsonian. Reflecting on this little hero in 1926, Harry Webb Farrington, a poet and preacher, described the pigeon: "Little scrawny blue and white, messenger for men who fight."

Messenger for men who make money, too. Stockbrokers and bankers relied on pigeons to carry news of the markets before there were telephones and the Internet. It hasn't always been pure sweet love that is sent down by the dove. They have been used in the service of the empire, for money, power, and war.

Pigeons were employed (though probably not paid) by the Great Barrier Pigeon Gram Service and Mr. Howie's Pigeon Post, a form of airmail between mainland New Zealand and the Great Barrier Island. Pigeons can carry up to 2.5 ounces on their backs. I don't know how much the message "This is the Messiah" would have weighed—probably less than that. I suppose it's possible that the dove at the baptism carried a papyrus prepared by God the Father. But it doesn't seem quite like God, somehow, to employ the pigeon post to send a message. It seems a little too obvious, straightforward, unequivocal—as if God is sitting somewhere on a cloud with a pen in hand.

The writers of Scripture, though a varied group, usually seem to have more imagination than that. More artists, often, than exactly historians, they choose rich, thick symbols that resonate throughout the text—sometimes subtly, sometimes not (lamb, lion, grapevine). Like the iconography of painters, the images resound on levels far deeper than the surface. The appearance of the spirit of God as a dove at Jesus' baptism can surely be read as something more profound than the pigeon post. The spirit of God appeared in bodily form like a pigeon. I don't think we'd be wrong to consider that.

THE SPIRIT OF LIFE

The author of John says he didn't include everything in his book (of course not—it's twenty-one chapters; and Jesus, so the story goes, lived for *thirty-three years*—that's less than a chapter a year), but he wrote what he wrote so that we may come to believe that Jesus is the Christ, "and that believing you may have life." Jesus comes so that we may have life, and have it abundantly—eternal life, actually, is what John calls it. Whatever that means, it doesn't sound like the kind of belief that would come from a can or a tube tied to a pigeon's leg. God's "message" in Christ isn't something you "get" by reading words on a piece of paper. It is God's spirit that will give us life (great big abundant overflowing life like a spring forever welling up, according to John). The Spirit hovers over the water in Genesis and creates life—lots of it; plants yielding seeds of every kind, trees bearing fruit of every kind, swarms of living creatures, sea monsters, everything that moves, every winged creature—swarms, swarming and creeping, fruitful and multiplying, fungi, membranes, bowels. Bulbs, suckers, and buds sending out runners and tubers splicing and crossbreeding. And God says this is good, very good—resoundingly good.

The dove has come to seem banal and bland and cutesy as far as Christian symbols go. It has come to represent something polite and petite and pure. Maybe this has worked to deprive us of a more robust view of the Holy Spirit. Isn't it sort of limiting to imagine the spirit of God as something dainty and white? We are made of dirt, according to the creation account in Genesis. We are full of bacteria. We each carry two to five pounds of bacteria in our bodies—two to five POUNDS. We could kill a dove with one or two blows from the back of our hand. We need a spirit that can handle us.

In *The Voyage of the Beagle,* Charles Darwin marvels at the "extreme tameness" of the doves he encounters on Charles Island. They are so easily killed by buccaneers and whalers and sailors who, he says, "always take cruel delight in knocking down the little birds." He describes a little boy he saw sitting at a well with a big pile of dead birds beside him. The boy sat at the well all day, says Darwin, with a switch in his hand, waiting to kill the birds when they came to take a drink.

Surely we need God's spirit to be less easily done away with—something that can handle the fungi, membranes, and bowels. Not some fragile naive princess dressed in white, unaware or untainted by the ways of the world.

GODDESSES OF LOVE

The dove in the lore of ancient civilizations wasn't, actually, quite so pure. The bird has a complicated past when you dig a little deeper. Ishtar, a sexy, promiscuous, violent Babylonian goddess, was often depicted as a dove. *Pure* and *naive* and *delicate* would not be good words to describe her. She's more of everything that pulls at humanity all rolled up into one: passion and jealousy and anger and sex. She's goddess of war, fertility, and love. In the Epic of Gilgamesh, which predates the biblical text, Ishtar pushes Gilgamesh to marry her. Although he may find her attractive, he declines because she's proved to be a bit much for her previous lovers, leaving them dead or maimed.

Gilgamesh says, "Listen to me while I tell the tale of your lovers." Then he goes on to describe how she broke the wing of one, dug pits for another, rustled up a whip and spur and thong for her stallion lover, struck her shepherd lover and turned him into a wolf, and "now his own herd-boys chase him away, his own hounds worry his flanks."

The ancient goddess dove was not a bird easily knocked down by whalers, sailors, and buccaneers, or a little boy with a stick.

In another story, Ishtar descends to the underworld looking for her lover. She's very threatening—knocking on the door to the underworld, screaming that she'll break, smash, wrench, force the doors if she isn't let in; and she will "bring up the dead to eat the living." When she does, finally, get in, leaving the face of the earth, all sexual activity ceases everywhere. Fertility dies. It's like she's necessary to life at the same time she threatens it. It's always interesting to see, when you start looking around at other gods and the founding narratives of other cultures, how different the Hebrew stories are. The God who hovers over the deep in Genesis speaks a word—no screaming, threatening, breaking, and smashing—no violence at all. There are no monsters slain, no battles fought. The spirit of God hovers and coos and the world is born, grows fertile, with hardly a bang. The spirit of God at creation is not violent, but God may not be a naive princess either.

Astarte, a Semitic goddess (representing fertility, sexuality, war); Aphrodite (love, beauty, pleasure, procreation); and Venus (same as Aphrodite) are all associated with doves. These goddesses all have many lovers—promiscuity being more their thing than purity. The dove was considered sacred to Adonis and Bacchus. In all these myths the dove was invested with erotic meaning. It became the symbol of love between humans and between the deity and its worshipers.

Pigeons are known for their sexual appetite. In order to get their pigeons to fly home fast and furious, competitive pigeon racers will sometimes make use of their tendency to be powerfully aroused. Some pigeon racers will place a couple together, allow them a certain amount of foreplay, and then pack one of the desirous pigeons up and drive it away. When released, the pigeon flies back home fast.

When pigeons mate they appear to kiss. They are actually

exchanging food, but it looks like they are making out (without lips of course—which does make it different). When they copulate, it is gentle and consensual (compared to, say, watching the geese at the park); and they make love frequently, any season of the year, and have many babies—sometimes as many as twelve batches a year. With all their zeal for sex, they are usually true to one love—mating for life.

They can also be quite the fighters. Of course they aren't predators, but they do pick fights with one another, sometimes their own mates. Anyone who watches them long enough in confined quarters might begin to wonder how they came to represent peace. They are not one simple thing—like humans, like the spirit of God. Maybe peace isn't one simple thing either.

GRAY

It's a wonder, with its colorful mythological history and randy nature, that the dove has become the symbol of purity.

A dove is a pigeon. That seems worth saying repeatedly. We may have imagined the dove at the baptism was white, but it was more likely gray, with an iridescent green-and-violet neck—a rock dove, which is very common in Palestine and which is considered to be the ancestor of our common domestic pigeon. The common domestic pigeon—the kind that gathers in our parks, nests in our eaves, poops all over our buildings and sidewalks.

Archaeological evidence suggests that the dove was domesticated very early in the history of humans. People have been raising them to eat and race and sacrifice and carry messages for a very long time (three thousand years at least, perhaps more). Archaeologists have dug up ancient underground pigeon coops all across Israel; some apparently held thousands and thousands of birds. Ruins of old coops have been found all across the world. The Romans sacrificed them to Venus. The Hindus fed them. The Europeans ate them by droves.

The rock pigeons found in our cities and barns are probably from populations established by escaped domestic pigeons. They are often referred to as feral pigeons. How is that for a symbol of the Holy Spirit? I believe it's a good one. I like it. It's ubiquitous, on the streets. The white dove is overused. How about pigeons for Pentecost, on banners and bulletin covers? There are lots of birds that want to avoid us, who are too wild for us, who need their space. You could call them unfriendly. Pigeons want to be close to us. They are where we are—in some of the worst places we have made (our neglected projects and abandoned buildings) and some of the best (art museums, parks, Rome's piazzas). They won't leave us alone.

Yet there's hardly a bird that people are more likely to want to shoot and exterminate. People are very often not fond of pigeons. They call them "rats with wings." They are considered pests who "infest" urban areas. Cities have tried countless ways of exterminating them, usually unsuccessfully. What if the spirit of God descends like a pigeon, somehow—always underfoot, routinely ignored, often despised?

We celebrate Thanksgiving at the dairy farm where my husband's grandparents lived out their entire lives. His sister lives there now. The cows are gone, but the pigeons remain. After dinner this year, Jim took me up to the hayloft. Pigeons were everywhere. It's always a little frightening to have a bird flap by your head in an enclosed space, but I have been reading so much about them, I am just happy to be among these birds. We sit and watch and listen. It sounds like hundreds of lovers have just been satisfied—the way they coo and moan. It is sweet and peaceful and animal. After a while, Jim tells me a story about the Christmas he and his brother got BB guns. They crawled up the ladder to this loft and shot pigeons. Jim says, "I still feel guilty. It's one of the few things I have ever killed." Later, my colleague the Reverend Russell (also a generally nonviolent man), confesses to fantasies of hauling out his grandpa's gun to shoot the pigeons that relieve their bowels all over his back porch.

The passenger pigeon used to be so prolific in North America that Audubon described flocks so large that they took three days to pass by, blocking out the sun. I learned this from Tom Waits when he called in to Bob Dylan's radio show. Early explorers describe "infinite multitudes," "countless numbers." It's estimated that they made up more than 45 percent of the total bird population in North America. This is hard to even imagine: the skies bursting with profligate life (like an ever-flowing spring, like eternal life, almost).

They were so abundant that Audubon, as well as countless others, saw no reason not to shoot them. They were hunted on a massive scale in the Midwest. Their characteristics (one blogger says their "stupidity") made them easy to slaughter. They all grouped together. They would even perch on one another's backs. Massed together like this, they were easily, quickly, and efficiently slaughtered. Their carcasses were loaded on to boxcars and shipped to the East, where they were sold as inexpensive food for slaves and the poor. In New York City in 1805, a pair of pigeons sold for 2 cents. The spirit of God—like cheap meat. The passenger pigeon went from being one of the most abundant species in the world in the nineteenth century to utter extinction in the early twentieth.

Maybe the spirit of God is so common—*wherever life is,* that we don't recognize it or necessarily respect it. And so we snuff it out sometimes. This does not seem entirely unlikely to me. Maybe this is the explanation—the explanation for why we are unkind, ungenerous, why we ever hate and kill one another. Why we are ungrateful and destructive. The spirit of God is among us, the Holy Spirit, and we often don't even notice it.

Maybe we don't notice because we are looking for something pure and white, but the spirit of God is more complicated than that—fuller and richer and everywhere. Perhaps we've read the dove wrong—it is not pure as the driven snow. Maybe we get a little hung up on purity. God, after all, created LIFE (everything swarming and creeping, fruitful and multiplying). Maybe the Holy Spirit of God is more creative than puritan. Maybe we are mistaken about what *holy* means.

PURITY LAWS

Some rabbinic writings suggest that the animals and birds that are forbidden to the Jews to eat are those that possess bad character traits. What a person eats has an effect on them; therefore, Torah forbade animals that would badly influence the people's character. The story of Noah illustrates the dove's good habits. Noah sent one out of the ark to test if the floodwaters had subsided. It consented to go without protest. "She did not permit her personal interest and desires to interfere with her mission." Some birds demonstrate selfish and heartless characteristics and thus are unsuitable to eat, but the "modest and compassionate" dove is good to eat.

Unfortunately for the pigeon/dove, it's "purity" and "cleanness" also made it the only bird that was acceptable for sacrifices. This may have been somehow good for its reputation, but in actual fact involved a lot of bloody slaughtering.

Ramban, a Jewish scholar in the thirteenth century, suggests that it wasn't actually for their moral virtue that these birds were chosen as the sacrificial bird, but because they were easy to catch. "Torah chose animals that feed at his crib, and that he need not take weapons against." They were chosen as the sacrificial bird because they were abundant and easy to kill.

The Bible describes in gory detail the process for dove sacrificing; the beheading, the de-blooding: the priest "shall bring his offering of turtledoves or of young pigeons. And the priest shall bring it to the altar and wring off its head, and burn it on the altar; and its blood shall be drained out on the side of the altar; and he shall take away its crop with the feathers, and cast it beside the altar on the east side, in the place for ashes."

The birds were acceptable for burnt offerings and sin offerings if the people could not afford to give a mammal. Women "unclean" from childbirth, women with their period, lepers, men with discharge, were to offer a lamb for a burnt offering and a young pigeon or turtledove for a sin offering—or just the birds if they couldn't afford the lamb. Whereas other sacrificial animals needed to be male and without blemish, not so with the dove.

In the first chapter of the first book of the Bible, God hovers over the water at creation. God—like a dove (perhaps). The dove is a messenger of hope in the story of Noah. Get in just a little bit further, and the dove is being beheaded and de-blooded. Droves and droves of dove bones and feathers piled by the altar having fed the sacrificial system. Perhaps, in spite of what we intend—we somehow keep killing the Spirit. And it keeps coming back again, inexhaustible. After all the burning and draining and killing, it's nice to see it alive and whole, fluttering at Jesus' baptism.

THE "HOLY" SPIRIT

The religious institution has always struggled with what it perceives as unclean (parts of the body, what comes from the body, discharge and blood, lepers and pregnant women). Hebrew patriarchs and church fathers clearly had a bit of trouble with the womb.

Tertullian insists on maintaining the belief that God became fully human in Jesus, though he is clearly disgusted by some of the implications. "Start with the birth itself," he says, "an aversion, the filth within the womb of the bodily fluid and blood, the loathsome curdled lump of flesh which has to be fed for nine months of this same muck. The womb." Somehow I get the feeling that the Spirit (like a dove) hovering over the deep, hovering over Mary's womb, didn't feel quite the same way about "the muck." The Spirit called the muck into being, so the story goes—God shaped it with God's hands. God reveals Godself most fully, the Christian church professes, not as a rational system or a set of ethics or an unchanging principle, not as some magisterial deity or a pure white light, but as a living, breathing, bodily being. This is admittedly weird, but continually beautiful.

Perhaps purity laws were more predecessors to good hygiene (in a prescientific age) than revelations of sacred truth. That ancient cultures developed such taboos is evidence of some rudimentary knowledge of what might prevent the spread of diseases (washing hands may have helped the Jews survive antiquity). These seem like good reasons for people to have ideas about purity and impurity.

But Jesus? He comes along and things get a little unnerving. It's a big deal that his disciples don't wash their hands. It's like the climax of his ministry in Mark, when he declares all foods clean. He says what goes into a man can't defile him—well, maybe, but it can kill him. Try eating Hemlock or Pufferfish. Jesus comes on the scene and immediately violates the boundaries—violates the system that set in opposition the clean and the unclean, pure and impure, holy and unholy: they were supposed to be kept separate. Jesus touches everything. More than touches; he inhabits. He's God in the flesh, so the Christian tradition proclaims. He breaks the rules in so many ways.

Some laws, some parts of the religious mechanism, were about doing things that would set you apart, as God is set apart: "Be ye holy as I am holy." Well, holy looks a little unusual when you look at Jesus Christ in the stories the Gospels tell. It's almost like reverse holy, the opposite of setting apart. Jesus is right off the bat eating with sinners, touching lepers. He takes water from the Samaritan woman. God incarnate arrives into the world from his mother's womb. He's not setting things apart—he's mixing it up, in his very being. God in the flesh seems like some sort of explosive revelation of nonseparation. The spirit of God—like a pigeon.

Cultural and religious systems are often about keeping order. What is unclean is what is out of place. Dirt is matter out of place—what is out of place is dirty. Mud in its place is okay—but it's not okay on the kitchen table. Trying to keep things clean is about trying to organize the environment. It's the feral pigeons, the ones that inhabit our cities, that seem wrong and dirty to us. We like mourning doves in the field.

Different cultures have different sensibilities about what dirty means. Mary Douglas, the influential British anthropologist, says, "There is no such thing as absolute dirt, it exists in the eye of the beholder." It almost seems like with the revelation of the spirit of God in Jesus, there is no dirt. There is nothing unclean. The eye of the beholder is so generous. The creator of life loves it—all of it.

Dirt, according to Douglas, is a sort of category for what blurs, smudges, contradicts, or otherwise confuses accepted classifications. Jesus, the spirit of God, the spirit pigeon/dove, blurs, smudges, contradicts; he opens the door and lets in the unfit: the sinner and the blind and the lame and the poor and the sick and the weak and the meek.

"AND THE HOLY SPIRIT OF GOD
WAS UPON HIM"

The yearning for rigidity is in us all—the longing for hard lines and clear concepts: stable order—the right place to put the right thing. But the search for purity, cleanliness, can lead to some not so great places. Like the Inquisition; like fascism, homophobia, antibiotic-resistant bacteria.

It seems like the desire for purity involves some incredible layers of deceit. In almost every culture human waste is considered unclean. It makes a lot of sense. But consider this story: in the Chagga tribe in Tanzania, when the men were initiated into the holy circle, part of the initiation was supposedly that their anuses became blocked for life. It was a pretense, obviously. Supposedly the holy men never needed to defecate ever again, unlike women and children, the unholy, who remained subject to this dirty bodily necessity.

Mary Douglas says, "Imagine the complications into which these pretenses led Chagga men." Catholics, Evangelicals, Christians, Muslims, Jews, environmentalists, pacifists, all have their own versions of "the pretenses of the Chagga men." On the other hand, Saint Francis of Assisi is said to have rolled naked in filth and welcomed his sister, death.

Being human is beautiful, mysterious, and scary. A lot of the time we seem to believe that there are many things about being human that are not okay: dying and sweating, aging and fragility—and we're afraid people will see some weakness or impurity leaking out of our pores. So we have to hide a lot and lie a lot—even to ourselves, and the deceit is often really destructive. We exclude and judge, and we're unloving of anything that deviates in ourselves or in other people.

There's something about the story of God becoming human, entering the body fully, touching all over everything unclean—eating, defecating, suffering, dying—that would seem, if anything, to free us from the need to pretend anything—to pretend that we're anything other than what we are. God created us and loves us in a very thorough way—that seems to be the thrust of the narratives.

Jesus starts out his ministry by being baptized. Baptism is a symbol of death and renewed life. It's a bold statement to begin with. Gods don't generally die—nor would they stoop to being baptized in the river with the masses of the ordinary.

To be alive involves a lot: suffering and taste buds and sweetness and muck. The spirit of God is not apart from this. It hovered over the deep and called out life. John the Baptist says he saw it descend as a dove—a pigeon. It lands, hovers, plunges, and coos; coming again and again, leaving its droppings on our sleeves. We can hit it with a stick all day long, but it keeps racing to us, desirous that we might open our hearts.

THE

PELICAN

SACRIFICE *and* GIFT

WITH FOUR FEET OF snow, twenty-below temperatures, and three thousand pastoral obligations to attend to, I discovered I could use my computer to watch birds. There are live streaming video cams, PBS documentaries, and YouTube videos about pelicans. I can evade everything mundane and watch pelicans in Minnesota in the winter. Who knew? The YouTube pelican video with by far the most hits is one shot by a tourist in St. James Park, London, of a great white swallowing a pigeon whole.

Pelicans are huge and heavy waterbirds with great expandable throat pouches (their most distinctive feature), and really long beaks (longer than the beak of any other bird ever, actually). In the video the pelican waddles over to where the pigeons are pecking at the tourist bread and it snaps up a pigeon in its enormous beak and clamps it down so the pigeon is entirely enclosed in the great throat pouch, which is now expanding and bulging with the pigeon flapping its wings madly and very visibly inside of it. My thirteen-year-old daughter, sensitive to the plight of small animals, pointed out that you could hear the pigeon chirping (the Spirit clamoring?). After what seems like an eternity of flapping and chirping and slow desperate suffocation, the pelican swallows the pigeon whole.

Thomas Aquinas wrote a hymn to be sung in gratitude after drinking from the Communion cup, praising our Savior: "O loving Pelican! O Jesu Lord!" Dante and Shakespeare use the image as well: Jesus Christ our Pelican. It seems funny to me. I am all for "different" ways of seeing Christ, different images of God, images that may knock you off the track you're used to being on. How do you really get to know, get intimate with, anything or anybody, if you never see them anew, if you believe you've comprehended them and there's no more to know—but a pelican?

In another video, this time in a state park in Florida, a pelican swims after two baby ducks. It gets one in its mouth, but the little duck escapes. It gets the other duck in its mouth. It escapes. The pelican pursues them relentlessly. The videographer wonders why the pelican, whose diet consists almost entirely of fish, was trying to eat the baby ducks. Someone on the message board replies, "He wasn't trying to eat the baby ducks. Pelicans are just jerks."

O loving Pelican! O Jesu Lord!

Gene Stratton-Porter, who wrote about the birds of the Bible in 1909, says, "Perching pelicans are the ugliest birds imaginable ... they are included, with good reason, in the list of Levitical abominations." Ornithologists have called them stupid and ponderous, undemonstrative and grotesque, gawky, awkward, comical. But anyone who has ever seen one airborne must admit that they are almost magically graceful when they fly. But still, it is a strange bird in which to see Christ.

Thomas Aquinas may have never seen a pelican torment a pigeon. He may not have spent much time watching real pelicans at all. His image of Christ as pelican was probably informed by the erroneous belief, illustrated graphically in medieval bestiaries, that the mother pelican pierces her body to feed her own blood to her children to keep them alive. It was almost certainly this image of sacrificial love that moved the poets to identify this bird with Christ.

Although there has often been a tendency in the Christian tradition to strictly divide "man" from "beast," and the natural world from supernatural truths, the medieval bestiary takes a different tack. Based, at least in part, on biblical verses like Job 12:7-10 ("Ask the beasts, and they will teach you; the birds of the air, and they will tell you; or the plants of the earth, and they will teach you; and the fish of the sea will declare to you"), the writers and illustrators of the bestiaries believed every animal, every rock, every created thing contained the breath of God, and so they were working through how to hear in the breath some meaningful word.

These old lavishly illustrated manuscripts describe beasts real and imagined, known and unknown—what is seen and what is on the edge of consciousness: unicorns and dragons, griffons and ant lions, basilisks, catoblepas (a beast with a head so heavy it can only look down), he-goats (a beast so hot that its blood dissolves diamonds), and cuckoos. Bestiaries were often included in Psalters and prayer books. People carried them around for personal contemplation. All these wild creatures, so the thinking went, had something to teach those who were faithfully paying attention.

We've gone through a lot of stages of knowing since these artists and prescientists endeavored to understand every living thing. We know they didn't (even remotely) have the facts down. There's a lot of sloppy science—actually, there's hardly any science at all—yet there's something about the exploration, the openness to truth, that is other than humanly constructed; the reverence given to the natural world, the wild imagination, that keeps me from dismissing the bestiaries as ignorant relics of the dark ages. I like them.

We have often staked our lives, and the life of the planet, on the anthropocentric notion that we alone as humans are the crowning glory of creation. The assumption that we are the epicenter of the universe has had an enormous influence in the history of civilization (which could hardly be called benign). We often loathe our animalness and believe that our salvation somehow depends on our transcending "nature," our nature, our animal bodies, our physical support system, the rest of creation.

This sort of narcissistic tendency hasn't always been a plus for the well-being (for the life) of the material world. If the natural world is mostly something to escape or transcend, why not strip-mine and clear-cut, use pesticides and herbicides, let the unenlightened—the "lesser" species—become extinct, die off? Who really needs the whooping crane, the pink-headed duck, the spectacled cormorant? We know what we need to know without them. This mode of belief hasn't always been a plus for our personal psyches either; we're afraid to know who we are: a species among species, mammals who are born and die and defecate.

Although the "lessons" the medieval theologians derived from the behavior of the beasts might seem silly or wrong to contemporary science-laden readers, I like the vital attention these Christians gave to the beasts—the curiosity with which they observed them—as if they were purveyors of some sort of wisdom or knowledge not readily accessed by humans—as if observing them might unlock some window we normally keep shuttered. Jesus says, "Consider the birds."

Origen, one of the church fathers, urges his readers in a sermon on Leviticus to "understand that thou hast within thyself herds of cattle…flocks of sheep and flocks of goats…understand that the fowls of the air are also within thee." We may not suffocate pigeons in our mouths, but we are animals and we do animal things. I have felt herds in my chest. I need water and sleep and wings. Surely there is something we can learn from the birds (and the beasts)—something about our humanity and inhumanity, what it is to be a creature/human/animal/alive. I want to listen to what the pelican has to tell me, but it is probably not what Aquinas heard.

Aristotle wrote one of the first histories of animals in 350 BCE (after which the bestiaries are modeled). He gave the pelican its name. Although his classification of every living thing in a hierarchy of being, a "ladder of life," has undoubtedly contributed to the human superiority complex; though he is a founder of patriarchy, sexism, and inequality, there is something compelling to me about imagining his process of gathering information. He doesn't have binoculars or research stations. He just barely has a sense of the scientific method, but he's looking and listening so intently, trying so hard to figure out what it all means.

He begins his project by noticing that there are animals with blood, and animals without blood. He moves on. "Some animals are stationary, some erratic," he says. "Stationary animals are found in water, but not on dry land," and, *by the way,* he says (I like this one): "The sponge appears to be endowed with a certain sensibility. The difficulty in detaching it from its mooring is increased if the movement to detach is not covertly applied." Clearly he spent some time watching sponges, overtly and covertly trying to detach them. I like that in a Greek philosopher. He says, "Other creatures seek their food in the nighttime loose and unattached."

By the time you get to the medieval bestiaries, they are a little less intent on careful observation—a little more concerned with finding some edifying moral lessons. Some animals teach by way of positive example; some might be better classified as sinner animals. Creatures that "seek their food in the nighttime loose and unattached" would undoubtedly be in the latter category (those floozies and philanderers!). The pelican, however, is very pious. In the medieval bestiaries you don't get anything much more beautiful, and pure, and Jesus. The mother pelican has the greatest love of all creatures for its offspring, so the story goes, because she sacrifices herself (pierces her own breast with her beak) to feed her children with her blood.

So the pelican, more than any other creature, became the symbol of Christ on the cross, shedding his blood—a symbol of the Eucharist. And the "Pelican in her Piety," as the image came to be known, is all over the place in ancient Christian iconography: on altars and chalices; in breviaries; on family crests; woven into tapestries; carved on monastery doors. The image lingers on—in tattoo form on the back of some "alternative" Christians, as a Christmas ornament for the tree in some Lutheran churches, on the Louisiana state flag and seal.

MISTAKES WERE MADE

Bird observers over time have come to understand that there is no "pelican in her piety." The mother pelican doesn't peck her breast to feed her young. It's an ancient misinterpretation. People can only guess what it was that propelled this read. Maybe it was because in some species of pelicans, the pouch turns a reddish color in the spring. Maybe it was hard to tell what was going on without binoculars. Maybe it's because medieval Christian thinkers were eager to find the moral of the story, and it seemed to them that sacrifice was the highest virtue. We need to read and reread, imagine and reimagine. Sometimes we need to let go of what we think and go back and look again.

If we were to reimagine the medieval bestiary for the twenty-first century, the image of a pelican soaked in oil might be a better one than the mother pelican piercing herself. After the Deepwater Horizon oil spill off the coast of Louisiana, the media released photo after photo after heartbreaking photo of pelicans drenched, immobilized, suffocating in the oil unleashed by the disaster in the Gulf of Mexico. The image became the unofficial icon of the environmental casualties of the fossil fuel industry. Anyone who's seen a photo of an oil-soaked pelican trying to raise its heavy wings, its beak open in seeming agony, wings spread, pinned down with the heaviness of the oil, might think it looks like a crucifixion. But it is definitely not "the pelican in her piety." It's a pelican suffering as a result of human activity.

If the pelican is a symbol of sacrifice today, it's not the loving mother feeding her young, but the life of the environment that is sacrificed to fuel the world's unsustainable addiction to a non-renewable form of power—oil. The medieval bestiary proclaimed the pelican a symbol emblematic of Christian charity. To look at it now, it might appear to be quite the opposite—a symbol of what we are willing to sacrifice to sustain our way of life, our habits, our cars—our species' tendency to keep expanding our territory pell-mell.

When the Deepwater Horizon rig exploded off Louisiana's coast on April 20, 2010, it unleashed more than 170 million gallons of crude oil into the Gulf of Mexico. Although we keep hearing that the disaster never materialized in the proportion predicted, the effect on pelicans and other birds isn't something that can be measured in the short term. Plenty of the oil-soaked birds died, but the oil also lapped into marshes and beaches where thousands of birds make their nests. Then there were the chemical dispersants sprayed by the thousands of gallons. As we should have learned by now from so many of our doings, you can't really alter the chemistry of the sea, air, or dirt without unforeseen results.

Many bird species affected by the Exxon Valdez spill in 1989 seemed to recover, only to see their numbers plummet in the decade following. The damage done by these sorts of environmental disasters can't really be determined by counting dead birds. The oil and the chemicals are something that could affect the pelican's fitness or longevity or reproductive ability for years to come.

It seems like some sort of cosmic irony that "the pelican in her piety" is featured on both the Louisiana state flag and seal. On the flag three drops of blood spill from the mother's breast as she sits above a ribbon with the state motto: "Union, Justice, and Confidence"—as if her sacrifice, each drop of blood, might sustain these noble ideals. It does not. Read and reread the story of Christ. Jesus didn't die to sustain our noble ideals but rather to show where our noble ideals can lead: we will kill to maintain our order, to preserve what we think is right. We find some *other* that stands in the way of our manifest destiny and crucify it.

MURDER OR SACRIFICE

In some medieval books of beasts, you get a variation of the pelican in her piety. The pelican is devoted to its children. But when the children begin to grow up, they flap their parents in the face with their wings, and though the pelican has great love for its young, it strikes back in anger and kills them.

Three days afterward, the mother pierces her breast, opens her side, and lays herself across her young, pouring out her blood over the dead bodies. This brings them to life again. "In the same way, our Lord Jesus Christ," says *The Book of Beasts,* a twelfth-century bestiary. The illustrations in this version show three distinct scenes: the babies attacking their parent; the parents killing the babies (one holding the necks down while the other strikes them); and finally, the one parent feeding the young by ejecting blood from its beak into the beaks of the young.

Somehow that doesn't seem quite like love. Murdering your children because you're angry at them, and then piercing your side to bleed on them to revive them, is not an act that could be classified as agape, phileo, or eros. It is the act of a repentant abuser. "In the same way, our Lord Jesus Christ"? I hope not. Humans have been venerating sacrifice as something necessary and beautiful and holy for a very long time. But perhaps exulting the pelican lacerating herself was as much a theological blunder as it was a zoological misread.

Sacrifice is a prehistoric activity, something that humans have been doing for a very long time. People offered their best crop or an animal, their children, all sorts of things, to the gods because they believed the gods required it. Sacrifices were offered to the gods so the gods wouldn't be angry and make famines and earthquakes, or so that the gods would be happy and make everything fertile. Sacrificing made people feel secure and safe—like they had done what needed to be done—like they were covered. Archaeologists have dug up vessels, carvings, the remains of animals and children that appear to have been "given" sacrificially to the gods across cultures and continents.

It wasn't just unusually cruel and awful people who sacrificed. Sacrifice is what kept the world going, what kept the world peaceful, people believed. The human condition is fraught with constant threats: starvation, attack, earthquakes, volcanoes, floods. It's scary. So people tried to find a way of negotiating with the gods to make it less scary. Sacrifice was like a form of exchange with the gods, a way of doing business. People across the religious spectrum were devoted to the sacrificial system.

The system lingers on. Of course we don't believe in throwing virgins off cliffs or offering our firstborn. We wouldn't think the pelican pious if she killed her children, no matter what her next move—we hardly believe in spanking. Yet most people believe deeply in the sacred character of sacrifice. We believe that someone must pay. We have to give up what is most dear to us to bring ourselves closer to God. Without pain there is no gain. If we are to create anything of value, sacrifices must be made. It is how the world works and we believe in its economy.

Of course we don't believe in child sacrifice, but our government officials comfort parents grieving the loss of their children to military conflicts with sacrificial rhetoric: they gave their lives for their country. It isn't just extremist groups that recruit young people to risk their lives. In his inaugural presidential address, President Obama spoke gratefully of "the sacrifices borne by our ancestors." He surely didn't mean to call up images of bloody goats on altars, but, still, he references an ancient system of blood for prosperity.

When the ancient potentates built a pyramid or fortress or temple, they often believed it would fortify, protect, or bless the structure to bury a child or a slave or a virgin in the foundation. For something to flourish, the thinking went, something else must die. The way we behave in the world (destroying wetlands for strip malls, old-growth forests for profit, songbird habitat for housing developments, pelicans for oil) would suggest we still believe in the truth of this system.

Sacrifice seems to move people. Not just the ancient writers of bestiaries, but people listening to presidential addresses, people watching reality television—where every episode includes the painful sacrifice of some for the advancement of another. The idea that something has to die (or bleed, or hurt, or suffer) in order for something else to live is an ancient and incredibly enduring belief. But perhaps it's the father of all lies more than the mother of truth.

GIVING WITH ABANDON

Over and over again in the Hebrew Scripture, we hear that God does not desire our sacrifice. We often assume that's because someone was doing it wrong or we take it as a condemnation of empty ritual, but then Jesus takes up the cry, seems to plead, "If only you had learned what this means: 'I want mercy and not sacrifice.'" As if having learned that, something vital might have shifted, something crucial might have been revealed. If we only learned what God desires, some bloody mechanism would break in the machine. Mercy not sacrifice. Imagine the beauty of the scene—some wild flourishing of life, instead of death for life. Scapegoats would not have to take the blame for the fact that none of us live up to our ideals. Those accused of witchcraft could come down off the stake—teach Aristotle about medicinal herbs. The gawky and awkward, the loose and unattached would not be shunned. There would be shiploads of children and soldiers and indigenous peoples, the maimed, the ostracized, the fat, and the sad alive and well among us. The dodo bird, the sea cow, the blue-footed booby, the pelican free of oil—grace in flight.

We're very much influenced by the idea that something has to die in order for something else, something better, to live. But maybe that isn't the desire of the Creator—everlasting-life-giver-lover-of-all-things. It was the other gods, the made-up ones, the false ones that required sacrifice; this God (Jesus is dying to show us) is a God of grace.

A lot of people say that the cross was the ultimate sacrifice. Maybe that's not a helpful or very true way to perceive the central activity of the incarnate God. Clearly sacrifice moves people, but maybe God wants to move people in an entirely different way. God's work in the world doesn't work like a business—like commerce or trade: give up this and you'll get that—blood for love, the death of one thing so that something else can live. It's a lot more creative than that. It's not tit for tat. It's grace upon grace upon mind-blowing grace.

Sacrificial rhetoric definitely serves the empire. How else would you raise armies and people your factories? It probably works out pretty well for the church sometimes (the belief that God loves a sacrifice). It might be good for business. But I don't think sacrifice makes us better lovers.

The veneration of sacrifice underlies a lot of Christian morality. The herds indulge, the goats stuff themselves with anything they can find to eat—Christians sacrifice their desires for a greater good. We put to death lust and gluttony and worldly desire and we gain purity or favor. The world indulges; Christians sacrifice. Questioning sacrifice seems like something only outlaws or rabble-rousers or Ayn Rand or Nietzsche or some hedonistic ego-driven fascist believer in the überman power-power would do. If you're a good person who cares about other people, you must believe in sacrifice. It's like it's written in the code of the universe. It's necessary for love, to raise children, to make marriage work, to avert environmental disaster. It seems like it resonates with every cause no matter which side you're on.

But maybe there's something flawed, something distorted and destructive, something non-life-giving in the rhetoric. Period. We need to stop using so much oil. We need to give to our children. We need to love the planet with a little more passion than we've shown. But maybe being attentive to the needs of the web of life that surrounds you isn't sacrifice. It isn't putting something to death; it's more like love—like learning to love with a little more passion, learning to give with a little more abandon. God wants to give us our hearts' desire—God just needs to work on our hearts a little.

Anyone who has ever had or been a child knows the last thing you want to hear from your parents is "I sacrificed for you." It's not what you want. It doesn't feel like love. You don't want them to give up their lives for you; you need them to be alive— the more fully alive, the better.

We've been so inculcated in the church with the idea that sacrifice is good and beautiful and necessary, it's a little hard to shift perspective—but maybe this is something that Jesus Christ our pelican is trying to get us to do. He isn't trying to reinforce the system; he is trying to undo it.

Sacrificing life equals death—not more life or better life. People have been sacrificing a long time: we've sacrificed wetlands, badlands, innumerable species, trees, mountaintops, salmon streams—believing somehow that this is what is necessary to make our lives better, or to get what we want or what we think we need. But it isn't working.

Sacrificing life equals death. Sacrifice is not a sustainable practice. It is not what the life-giving Creator God is after. This is an important shift to make—not just for atonement theory or biblical studies, but for the life of the planet.

Sacrifice isn't what's required to make something good and valuable, but maybe joy is. Maybe gratitude and compassion are essential. Sacrifice is essential to the empire of death but not in the kingdom of God. What God gives is always in the form of gift, not exchange. It's hard to imagine a world without sacrifice, without something having to die in order for something else to live. It is outside any economy we've ever known. But it might be worth imagining: some crazy/beautiful flourishing of life and more life and more life—eternal life—God giving with abandon.

Jesus says, "Go and learn what this means, 'I desire mercy, and not sacrifice.'" That seems like a hopeful direction to go. It seems like a hopeful thing to try to find out—to be pointed toward. When Jesus says, "This is my body, which is given for you," it seems like he means for us to understand it as a gift. It isn't business as usual, sacrifice as usual. It isn't God giving up what God loves: it is God's love, and it is very passionate. When we drink from the Communion cup we accept a gift— a big one, a world-changing one. The cup contains a lot: bones and blood and death and feathers—it's big and wide and deep.

WATCHING PELICANS FEED

Watching a pelican feed its babies is kind of a wild scene. It certainly is something that would catch a person's eye. The parents fly all over—sometimes sixty miles back and forth—to find food for their children. I'm not sure I understand exactly how this works, but apparently they eat the fish then they get back to the nest and they regurgitate the fish into their pouches and the babies reach their whole entire heads into the mother's or father's pouch to try to get the food. It looks uncomfortable. Especially if you're a human and you're thinking what it would be like if you had two babies putting their entire heads inside your mouth.

The children seem utterly voracious and desperate, like they have no idea how intent the parents are on feeding them. They seem afraid of not getting enough food. The whole thing *looks* kind of like a fight. But the parents aren't fighting them—they're feeding them. The children fight one another sometimes. If they are somewhere where the food is scarce, fratricide is not uncommon. The bigger chick kills the littler chick. But this is not the work of the parent.

There is another very peculiar pelican feeding behavior: the babies are all wrestling crazy around to get the food, sticking their heads into the parents' mouths, and then sort of suddenly, they faint. No one knows why they do this, whether they've lost oxygen by doing the head-in-the-mouth thing, or what. But they all do it. Fall on the ground like they're dead. It would be hard to know what was going on without the voice-over in the *Wild Planet* episode. It might look, in all the chaos, like the parents killed them. Maybe if Aristotle saw this in 400 BCE, that's what he thought was happening, but it was a misread.

To know the surface of something is to barely know it at all, and everything can be seen from different angles: an idea, a tree, a pelican could look different every day. We interpret and we reinterpret constantly. Sometimes an interpretation really settles in—that doesn't mean it couldn't stand to be unsettled.

ON THE BEACH

Pelicans may indeed be listed as an abomination in Leviticus, but watching a group of them skirt the waves on an overwhelmingly condo-laden beach in Florida, I feel like they are what redeems the abomination. They are incredibly graceful. Dinosaurlike. In fact, paleontologists have found fossilized remains that suggest that pelicans exist now in pretty much the same form as they did thirty million years ago. Thirty million years. They are largely silent creatures, gliding through our structures, watching us as if we don't always know what we are doing—and yet they are unperturbed by the ruckus we create:

O loving Pelican! O Jesu Lord! I try to focus on them and believe that perhaps, humans aren't capable of destroying God's creation—that we might finally quit abiding by the sacrificial system, keep trying for the possibility of life lived not at the expense of other life. I watch the pelican and glimpse the possibility that God's endless creativity and mercy will keep sustaining the world.

T H E
QUAIL

D E S I R E
and S L A V E R Y

I HAD BEEN THINKING and reading about quail for weeks when my friend Linda and I ended up at Cosmos, one of the many fine locavore-ish restaurants in Minneapolis. We get off the farm for our annual holiday splurge—tell our families we are going Christmas shopping in the city, but mostly we use the opportunity to go out to eat, stay in a nice hotel, talk, and drink wine. Quail is on the evening's menu. I have not seen quail on many menus—so I'm excited but a little reluctant. I have been reading Numbers 11, where the Israelites wandering in the wilderness are sick of manna and begin to crave meat. God says, "You want meat? I'll give you meat 'until it comes out of your nostrils.'" God sends a wind that blows in quail—tons of them, piles and piles; two cubits deep and as long as "a day's journey" on either side of the camp. The people gather the quail to eat, but "while the meat was still between their teeth," the people were struck dead by a plague and died.

This story doesn't make quail seem very appetizing, but quail is right here on the menu, paired with a Chardonnay. And wanting to somehow get more in touch with those newly freed Israelites, of course I order it.

It is a very little breast, white and delicate—seared with a cranberry vinegar reduction. It is gone in two bites. I like it. Linda, on the other hand, has to leave the table to vomit. I'm not making this up. The quail does not come out of her nostrils, and it is probably from a seafood allergy (there was fish in the amuse-bouche) or too much wine—not the quail, but still. We have been planning to see Andrew Bird in concert after dinner. Linda is too sick to go, so I go alone.

I know I probably shouldn't make much of this, but for a moment I forget and I think it is a sign from God, even though I don't know what it could possibly mean. It's just an odd coincidence, but I can't help telling everyone I know ("I was just reading about the Israelites vomiting because they ate too much quail and then Linda and I went out to eat and there was quail on the menu and we ate it and she vomited and she was too sick to go hear Andrew Bird")—so, I guess I did make something of it, though I'm not sure what exactly.

If nothing else, it made me keenly aware that it might be best not to stand apart and condemn the Israelites' clamoring for meat, but rather, recognize myself, my friend, the human condition in them. It makes me think long and hard about what my friend and I desire, *how* we are hungry and *what* we are hungry for—how even amid tall buildings and soft cushions and decorative lights, even with the attentive waiter, we are like the

Israelites wandering in the wilderness, ratcheted about by our desire, wanting more, or wanting something different. We are driven by desire, flattened by desire—desire is *huge*. Standing on the floor at First Avenue, watching Andrew Bird alone, I desire to be six feet tall, instead of five—I want to be able to see in the crowd. I want to be with my friend.

DESIRE

People have been thinking about what desire is and what we should do with it from many different angles for a very long time. The Buddha said that it is our cravings that make us suffer, and we can get beyond suffering by recognizing our desires and then letting them pass without attaching ourselves to them. The Sufis say the renunciation of desire is a step on a path that will eventually lead you back to longing, but when you get back to it, your craving will be for God. The Greeks believed it was all about keeping it in check. Kant opposed reason and desire. The romantics embraced it.

Augustine believed the root of evil is inordinate desire. It is the fleeting attraction of transient passions. He contrasted true happiness in life with the pursuit of lustful pleasure. But Augustine also said that God uses our misplaced desire to draw us, in spite of ourselves, to Godself. In our desire for beautiful things, we are unexpectedly drawn by God's beauty, which God describes as seductive. God seduces us by attracting our desire.

I learned what was supposed to be a pretty simple lesson in Sunday school at the Bible Baptist church where I grew up: there are godly desires and there are worldly desires. You were supposed to encourage the one and squelch the other in order to live a good and fulfilling life. I appreciate the attempt to sort this all out, but I have not found it to be that simple. I'm not sure desire can be sorted out quite that neatly. It's Christmas. Everybody is caught up in some incredible tangle—we don't want to be sucked into vacuous consumerism, we want to make our kids happy, we want to resist, we want to indulge, we want to contemplate the Incarnation, and we want to make beautiful packages. You can think about it long and hard and still not know what your desire is. Contemplation, meditation, feeling-more-than-thinking may help you find it, but this takes a lot of practice—day after day after day.

I'm pretty sure Linda and I go on our annual Christmas outing in some part because we desire an escape from monotony (driving to work, cleaning the kitchen, washing towels). I imagine, just like the Israelites, I would get tired of manna, tired of eating the same thing day after day. According to the psalmist, manna was the "bread of the angels," but what is that? Whatever angels are, they are not like me. I realize "bread from heaven" is a good metaphor, but it doesn't sound like something I actually want to eat. I like what grows in the dirt, ancient vines. I like the meat of animals and what grows on trees. Angel food sounds bland. I realize I should probably desire angel food, but I don't.

Desire is huge and complicated. We long and we lack and our longing and lacking make us create beautiful paintings and poetry. It draws us to one another. We don't just grow turnips—we desire more, so we grow heirloom tomatoes and spicy basil.

We long for something other than processed food so we make organic gardens.

On the other hand, people do get sick trying to fulfill their desire. We hurt people and we wreck things. Desire for profit has made this country sick. It is like a plague. We desire more wealth, try to gather it up, but people are dying without health care and jobs. The rivers and lakes are toxic. The next generation may have it far worse than we can even imagine, but "the meat is yet in the teeth" of the 1 percent.

When the Israelites were tired of wandering through the desert, hungry and complaining, God gave them (as the psalmist puts it) "their own desire." Manna is on the grass in the morning and quail fly into the camp every evening. The piles of quail are knee high, and yet no one is exactly satisfied.

God gives us what we need—ground and water, light, food, birds, blood, breath—and it could all stop there, and we could just be grateful, but doesn't God also give us desire?

When we started out it seemed like Linda and I were simply going to have a nice meal. It was an annual event that was easy to read: friends have fun. But then the Bible story came in, and suddenly the whole thing became full of disparate meaning. Maybe this is the point of Bible stories. When you are immersed in them, they get you thinking. Even if you can't pinpoint a lesson, even if the meaning is ambiguous, it's still a gift. The Scripture infuses life with another layer of interpretation. The Scripture makes the moment pregnant. Linda agrees, not even reluctantly, even though she is the one who vomited quail into the hotel toilet.

FOOD

I can't see wild quail where I live in Minnesota. The northern bobwhite is rare here, although it used to be plentiful in southern Minnesota. We have plowed and bulldozed much of its habitat. We have killed with herbicides the native plants the quail hide in and feed on. I can't see them running around, but I can eat them.

People have been devising ways to catch birds to eat as long as people have been alive—with traps, nets (some made from human hair), and boomerangs. Liming is still popular, though illegal, in the Mediterranean. It involves coating tree or shrub branches in a sticky substance so that when birds land on it they are immobilized and later gathered and cooked. People eat songbirds (robins! warblers!) in Cyprus and Italy. On Cyprus the illegal dish is known as *ambelopoulia*. In Italy it is *pulenta e osi*—polenta with little birds. Sailors stranded in the Arctic have been known to try eating penguin. We eat the symbol of the Holy Spirit—roast squab with bacon and grapes.

But by far the most common birds for eating are the gamebirds (the Galliformes order), which dwell on the ground, fly less heartily, and get fat. My friend Diane, who lives with us on the farm, studied ornithology before she had kids and became a nurse practitioner. She did her master's thesis on the function of song rate and repertoire size in red-eyed vireos. In her younger days she traveled the world doing bird research—counting bowerbirds in Australia, spotted owls in the Northwest. She released peregrine falcons into the wild in Colorado. She is the greatest lover of birds I know. I asked her what she thought about quail. She said, "I kind of think they're boring." The most memorable encounter she had with them, she says, was when she fed them to the peregrine falcons. She didn't mean to denigrate them, she said; "Of course they have a purpose, but I really love the birds that make it against the odds, through difficult circumstances, hard places. Quail are easy to domesticate and cheap to raise. They flourish in their domestication. I think of them mostly as a food source."

The *Encyclopedia of Life,* "a massive database bringing together trusted information from resources across the world," has a webpage for every species. It lists ways that people benefit from each particular type. Under the listing for the common quail, the importance for humans is listed as "pet trade / food." If I were a quail, I might find this insulting.

My first encounter with a real quail in the course of working on this chapter was in the restaurant in an urban center on my plate, not in the fields or the woods. Quail are raised domestically all over the world for both meat and eggs. Many quail farms advertise processed quail. This made me think of bologna, but it mostly means that they've taken the bones out. You can buy them frozen, wrapped in bacon, and vacuum-packed. This seems vaguely diminishing for a species.

For the Israelites the quail came with the wind—something wild blown in, but still they were primarily food. The Israelites don't wonder at their flight and feathers, or contemplate their significance. They eat them. The quail fulfill their hunger. What are they hungry for?

MORE THAN CALORIC CONTENT

In *The Art of Eating*, M. F. K. Fisher writes:

People ask me: Why do you write about food, and eating and drinking? Why don't you write about the struggle for power and security, and about love, the way others do? They ask it accusingly, as if it were somehow gross, unfaithful to the honor of my craft. The easiest answer is to say that, like most other humans, I am hungry. But there is more than that. It seems to me that our three basic needs, for food and security and love, are so mixed and mingled and entwined that we cannot straightly think of one without the others. So it happens that when I write of hunger, I am really writing about love and hunger for it, and warmth and the love of it and the hunger for it . . . and then the warmth and richness and fine reality of hunger satisfied . . . and it is all one.

God sends manna and quail to the hungry Israelites—it's food, obviously, but these stories are not just about protein and carbohydrates. We are complex creatures whose needs are not easily sorted into categories. One of the first comforts we find after we are thrust from the instant gratification of the womb is food—our mother's breast. It is not as immediate as the umbilical cord, but it is comfort, food, and security all rolled into one. We are incapable at this point in our lives of scavenging or hunting—we can't even hold our heads up on our own. We are completely and utterly dependent on our caretaker for food. Our very first experience of being cared for is being fed.

The Scripture is full of language that describes our relationship to God as food: "Taste and see how good the LORD is!" "My whole being thirsts for God." "Your word is so pleasing to my taste buds." "Hearken diligently to me, and eat what is good, and delight yourselves in fatness." "Whoever comes to me will never go hungry." Et cetera, et cetera.

Saint Francis de Sales likens the mystical state of union with God to a

> child still at the breast, whose mother, to caress him whilst he is still in her arms, makes her milk distill into his mouth without his even moving his lips. So...our Lord desires that our will should be satisfied with sucking the milk which His Majesty pours into our mouth, and that we should relish the sweetness without even knowing that it cometh from the Lord."

As M. F. K. Fisher said, "The warmth and richness and the fine reality of hunger satisfied...it is all one."

Clearly the folks wandering in the wilderness have not yet reached the mystical state of union. They are freed from slavery in Egypt, but they barely even celebrate before they begin to get hungry and thirsty. Bodily need is not something that is on the sidelines in these narratives. It is their throats and their stomachs that keep reminding them of their need for God in the desert. Their hunger is a risk they acquired when they were set free. Will God feed and care for them now? Was it God's love that led them to freedom and wandering, or is it that God hates them and brought them out to the desert to die? They struggle repeatedly with this insecurity.

They demand food and water, but what they really seem to need is the confidence that God is truly with them. Is the wandering meaningful or futile? Would it have been better to stay in Egypt where things were at least predictable? Should they really be following God in the desert, or are they fools to be doing so? It's a legitimate question. I've asked it myself on many occasions.

EXODUS: NICE GOD

In the midst of the wandering and wondering, the quail come as food. They appear twice—once in Exodus, later in Numbers. In the quail story in Exodus, the Israelites have just been liberated, but they almost immediately question the wisdom of leaving Egypt. They ask Moses sarcastically, "Is it because there are no graves in Egypt that you have taken us away to die in the wilderness?" They say, "Would that we had died by the hand of the LORD in the land of Egypt, when we sat by the fleshpots and ate bread to the full; for you have brought us out into this wilderness to kill this whole assembly with hunger." They have, after all, been "delivered" to wander in a desert wilderness where there is not much food or water and they have to camp and it is cold at night and it is hot in the day and they don't know how long they will be there. When the kids ask, "How much farther?" they can't possibly answer. No one knows. God never says. It turns out to be forty YEARS. The children have asked, "Are we there yet?" a million times, and by the time they get "there," most of the children are dead. It's a long time to travel. It is a lifetime. The wilderness is decidedly *not* the womb.

The people are never really sure about what's going to happen next. They seem scared and nervous. What about water? What about food? I don't blame them at all. They are no longer slaves in Egypt, it is true, but are they loved? Will they be taken care of? Will they ever rest again at their creator's breast? Sometimes they get a reputation for being whiners, but I can only imagine that I would be worse.

This "God" led them out of Egypt, but they don't trust him yet—they didn't really know him that well. He (if "he" is even a very good way of putting it) is a bit enigmatic, after all. Who can blame them? Will God provide for what they need now? There was a dramatic delivery, but what about sustenance? How is this God going to behave in the day-to-day? It's one thing to part water and do miraculous big hero-type things; it's another to provide sustenance. And why wouldn't there be an underlying suspicion of the god of the violent and the dramatic delivery? This God sent a plague that killed little Egyptian babies. There might be reasons not to trust a god that behaves like that.

In the Exodus story, God responds immediately to their needs and insecurity in a really beautiful way. They are hungry. They are worried about being cared for. God says, "Behold, I will rain bread from heaven." *Rain* is a good word to hear in the desert. So is *bread from heaven.* And not only that, meat, too! The Lord said to Moses, "I have heard the murmurings of the people of Israel; say to them, 'At twilight you shall eat flesh, and in the morning you shall be filled [*filled!*] with bread; then you shall know that I am the LORD your God," a good, kind, loving God who will take care of you. In the evening quail came and filled the camp, and in the morning the manna appeared.

In the Hebrew, the word used for the birds, *selaw,* means "fat." French cooks can't praise quail's tender white breasts enough. People in many times and places have eaten many kinds of birds. The sailors stranded in the Arctic who tried to eat penguins found that the meat was barely edible. They needed meat, and penguin was the meat that presented itself to them. But God sends the Israelites a delicacy—abundantly. The people need food and God provides it lavishly. Here the quail seem like such a gracious gift—almost over the top. We could have survived on Clif Bars—we get succulent delights.

There is a hint, though, that the people don't trust God yet. Some collected more manna then they needed for a day, and it "became infested with worms and stank." It is very hard to believe that God will provide what we need, even in the face of all the beauty of the earth.

NUMBERS:
GOD BEING A LITTLE MORE DIFFICULT

When the quail appear in Numbers, it's a different story (or, some suggest, a different version of the same story). In this version the people have been eating manna for a long time, and they have begun to find it monotonous. They are sick of manna and they want meat—meat like they ate in Egypt. They also want cucumbers and garlic and onions and melons like they ate in

Egypt. In the desert, people fantasize about juicy things. Cucumbers and melon seem better than the flaky white substance God's providing. This is not hard to understand. It takes a lot of practice to be grateful for what we have—especially when it isn't especially succulent. The Israelites don't have a lot of practice—they have just started their journey.

This story is often read as if it is a simple moral tale of greed and where greed leads. The Israelites have all they need in the wilderness. They have manna. They are fed—but they want more. They are still hungry after their bellies are full. God is angry about this, so he sends the quail to make them sick and to even kill them. The Israelites had too much desire, they didn't keep it in check, so they were punished. I'm not sure if this is a helpful way to read.

When the psalmist reflects on this episode, he says, "[God] gave them their own desire." What they are desiring at the moment is not just more, more, more—some unspecific "more." What they are fantasizing about is the food of their slavery.

They remembered eating well in Egypt, sitting by fleshpots—like it was all good back then, before they started their journey, before they wandered. It was so simple back there, with the cucumber and the melons and the fleshpots. Maybe the problem here is not so much that they desire too much, but that out there in the desert, they remember wrong—they are deluded.

They desire the food of their slavery. Do they really remember that they were filled with good food in Egypt? They weren't even given straw to make bricks. The pharaoh, their master, the "god" they served back in Egypt, didn't actually feed them well—

they were enslaved by him. Their desire may not be inordinate as much as it is wildly misplaced. When the quail come, it is not a delicacy in Numbers. It is oppressive. They demanded the food they craved? God gave it to them and it killed them.

When the ancient rabbis combed these texts, they saw that in Exodus the manna tasted like wafers made with honey. In Numbers it was like "cakes baked in olive oil." From this they concluded it was a miraculous food that could assume any taste a person desired. If someone in the family wanted meat—it would taste like steak. If your four-year-old wanted macaroni and cheese, it would taste like macaroni and cheese. You want something cheap, fleeting, and meaningless—something vacuous, like cotton candy? You want to eat the food of your oppression? Have at it, but it might not be very good for you. It might not give you much life or nutrition or vitality or a capacity to love and think.

COTURNIX COTURNIX

The birds in the story are probably the common, or Old World quail (*Coturnix coturnix*), as these would be the sort of quail the people writing the stories would be familiar with. Unlike the quail in the New World, these birds migrate. They fill up in winter on food in the south and then begin their trek through the Holy Land. Although they have more flight capacity than many quail, they are not like eagles or pigeons or birds that soar through the skies seemingly heedless of impediment. Quails needing to cross long distances often wait for a wind, because they tire easily. Migration is an effort. When they need to cross a large body of water, they wait for the wind to blow in the direction they need to go. Otherwise, they might not make it across. They would fall from exhaustion and drown. "Pliny writes of their coming into Italy in such numbers, and so exhausted with their long flight, that if they sighted a sailing vessel they settled upon it by hundreds and in such numbers as to sink it. Taking into consideration the diminutive vessels of that age and the myriads of birds, this does not appear incredible," says Gene Stratton-Porter in her *Birds of the Bible*.

I can see how one could interpret such a large number of birds in varying ways. I've just watched a swarm of starlings converge on the tree in front of my office, fly wildly, then converge again. There are so many. They are beautiful at a distance, but a little creepy en masse nearby. How you interpret them depends on your angle: a gift from God, a plague of pests, the Holy Spirit, rats with wings.

Quail are usually well camouflaged; they have markings that make them blend in with grasses and the shade of grasses. They trust in their camouflage, so they often sit still instead of running or flying to avoid predators. This usually works for them. When something gets too close, they might first try running, and then try bursting into flight. These bursts are sudden and rapid and short, and they are startling to the predator, or the person out for a walk. I've experienced this sort of behavior with pheasants many times. They aren't fast or strong, but they might give you a heart attack.

Quail are often interpreted as helpful and friendly. Clearly they are not imposing or ominous. Galen, a second-century physician and philosopher, called quail "the casualty of thunder." He claimed that the gall of the bird was helpful for a headache and the blood was helpful for an earache. Pseudo Galen, in his medieval pharmacology, wrote, "If the cruel person eats from the heart of this bird, he becomes friendly, because its heart turned his cruelty into friendliness." In some cultures quail are considered to be good signs. For example, if you are walking on an isolated road or path in the woods and suddenly a quail appears in your path, you know a friendly person will show up in your life. Newly married couples in Lithuania eat quail for good luck in their marriage. In France, a bridegroom carries the heart of a male quail and the bride the heart of a female quail to ensure happiness in their life together.

In other cultures they mean trouble. The quail is taboo in Madagascar. In Hungary it is an accursed bird. An ancient pharmacopoeia records the odd idea that quail were transformed frogs that had eaten gourds and that they could change into rats. Medieval bestiaries claimed they were poison, but Aristotle in his *Animalia* observed that they were actually able to eat what is normally poison (hemlock, henbane, and hellebore) without negative effect. Thus they became symbols of protection. It's no wonder that the Bible is a little ambivalent about what the quail means: gift or curse? toxic or nutritious?

BLUNDERING LOVERS

You get the feeling throughout the stories of the Hebrew people that they are just getting to know Yahweh, just learning to trust and love God. We often think of the wanderers as ungrateful, unfaithful, barely conscious. But maybe they are just learning what it is to be free. And it isn't that simple to be free. They are not yet wise. Their desires are not yet matured. This, after all, is just the beginning of their narrative. They don't even know who God is yet. We are not so different.

There's no logical or geographical reason for it to take forty years to get from Egypt to the Promised Land. We sometimes believe the shortest path is the best one, but maybe (God knows) there is a need to wander. There is unmapped territory that needs to be explored—desires to be let go of, renounced, or transformed. God's seduction is not a crass come-on, nor is it smooth. The path to intimacy may be long and complicated.

Between the story of quail in Exodus and the story of quail in Numbers, God repeatedly calls the Israelites a "stiff-necked" people, implying a sort of rigidity. God calls them this in reaction to their worshiping the golden calf, a move that is often seen as the opposite of stiff—they are too loose, fickle, inconstant, easily infatuated, and impatient. Their hunger is out of control. But in the story God seems to sense that this move represents something else: they are stuck in some old way of seeing and doing and being, like there hasn't even been an exodus from Egypt—like all they know of gods are statues and tyrants. They don't have the imagination for a living, loving God who can be trusted. They edge in and out of this all during the sojourn, claiming God hates them—promised them liberation, only to lead them out into the wilderness where he will kill them. They don't trust God yet. They have old ideas, undeveloped ideas—

they haven't rid themselves of the notions about gods they learned in Egypt.

God in these stories seems to be a bit of a blundering lover as well—at moments he could be gracious and tender, at moments (Moses points out at Mount Sinai) he could be perceived as doing evil. The narratives about him are mixed—like traces of an oppressive tyrant remain next to images of gracious love.

At Mount Sinai, God is a consuming fire, yet Moses climbs the pathway through the thick darkness, gets right up next to the consuming fire, and stays there for forty days. I'm not saying he got comfortable with God, but you do get the feeling that the two established some sort of intimacy. Moses certainly gets to the point where he's not afraid to talk back—ask questions. "Why," he says, "are you angry with the people you freed?" Rabbi Abbahu said, "If this were not written in the text, it would be impossible." Such audacity. It's almost like Moses is trying to coach God through the relationship: Don't act out of anger. Remember your promise. Remember love—because you're on the edge here, man, on the edge of being perceived as evil.

And it seems that God is open to what Moses has to say—*open*—neither tyrant nor statue. God says, "Let me alone that my wrath may burn against them." As if this is possible only if God is alone. Maybe he hopes that Moses won't leave him alone. Maybe God does not actually want to be left alone.

In the quail story in Exodus, God seems loving and gracious. God wants the people's trust and love. They are hungry? God will provide a banquet. They are thirsty? God will make water flow. In

Exodus the quail are a succulent treat—God's gracious response to the people's need. In Numbers God's anger is kindled and his fire burns when the people long for the meat of Egypt. And Moses at this point is frustrated too. Instead of advocating for them, he says, "Did I conceive all these people? Did I give birth to them, that you would say to me, 'Carry them at the breast, as a nurse carries an unweaned child,' to the fertile land that you promised their ancestors? Where am I to get meat for all these people?" Moses is so frustrated and tired and overworked that he gets a little dramatic. "If this is how it's going to be," he says to God, "please kill me."

God helps Moses. He divides the responsibility among more men—the elders. God tells Moses to gather seventy men and then God will come down and talk to them. God is concerned for Moses. God doesn't want Moses to have to bear it alone. He's going to help.

But then there's the meat part. God says to tell the people, "The LORD will give you meat, and you shall eat. You shall not eat one day, or two days, or five days, or ten days, or twenty days, but a whole month, until it comes out at your nostrils and becomes loathsome to you, because you have rejected the LORD who is among you."

God is angry because he has been rejected, and God is frustrated on Moses' behalf. You might glimpse a tyrant from one angle, but from another the God who passionately desires to be in relationship with his people, a God who feels vulnerable— who doesn't want to be alone. God desires God's people. They desire Egypt. God is deeply affected.

God gives the people what they desire and it kills them. The

Israelites bury the people who died from their craving and move on. The covenant between God and God's people somehow endures through the mess of anger and hurt and passion.

LUST AND GREED OR THANATOS AND EROS

The Israelites are routinely condemned by commentators and preachers for being greedy—for lusting for more than they have. But perhaps the real problem is that they are too rigid—they lack imagination. In these stories they are occasionally still playing slaves to the tyrant.

Perhaps the Midrash—that dynamic, multileveled Jewish, rabbinic engagement with Scripture—is on to something. The manna could have tasted like whatever the people wanted it to taste like, whatever they imagined—and all they can imagine is the illusory meat they got in Egypt. The quail coming as the fulfillment of this desire don't have a chance of feeding them nutritionally. The fulfillment of this desire is not life, certainly not too much life—it is death. These founding biblical narratives are stories of people beginning to discover what they need.

We might like to think of ourselves as autonomous beings who get to decide who we are going to be, but we are likely much more malleable than we think. We are often defined by the structures that keep us captive. In some ways our desires are so socially constructed that they can't rightly be called our own.

It makes sense that people whose imaginations have been confined and defined by empire might need a time of wandering in the wilderness to get free. Maybe the problem with the wanderers is not that they desire too much, but that they desire too little—or their desire lacks imagination. They are learning—but it is a winding path. It is not fast and there are switchbacks. At times they revert to Egypt instead of growing into something gorgeous. At other times they are grateful and they learn to love.

The stories aren't simply (it isn't simple) about greed and lust—they are about desire that must undergo transformation—desire that must be directed to life instead of to slavery.

PRAYER

The wanderers seem delusional when they say they want to be back in Egypt, but maybe that they are even able to articulate their desire for Egypt was a way to get free from it. At the end of the quail story in Numbers, we learn that the place where they encamped became known as "the grave of craving."

James Alison (a Catholic priest and theologian whom I admire a great deal) did a retreat for our church where we talked about prayer. He said prayer is the place where we allow our desires to be reached by God. We should not force our children to pray for the poor if what they really long for is chocolate pudding. To do so would be to induct them into the world of hypocrites.

In prayer we own up to our desires, Alison said, whether or not they seem acceptable. It is not helpful to hide—to pretend what we want is what we ought to want instead of what we really want but we can't mention. When you don't admit you want things—it runs you. It is only when you can bring together the words *I* and *desire* that what you want becomes alterable.

In prayer, Alison says, we open ourselves to the one who

wants to give us desire that will lead to life, freedom from slavery, love, relationship—intimacy. God does not desire to repress or oppress us, but rather to bring us more fully to life.

The structures that keep us captive are often fueled by a notion of scarcity—the belief that there is not enough to go around. Capitalism is dependent on this. We will get what we need only by competing. Our rivals (our neighbors, our friends, even our spouses) become our enemies because we're so hungry and we think there's not enough food.

Faith, on the other hand, says Alison, requires the imagination for the goodness of someone—the goodness of a God who has so much love that it is infinite. Faith is the imagination for abundance. Alison urges us to have daring imaginations—to risk desiring more. God doesn't want us to desire less; God wants us to desire more. But the capacity for wanting bigger and better things will come from our owning our desire for chocolate pudding. In the degree with which you imagine the goodness—that is the degree in which you will be given. We will always get what we want—that's the trouble: quail that tastes like grace, quail that tastes like slavery, quail that makes us vomit. But, says Alison, "we are being given imagination. Trust this."

THE PATH TO FREEDOM

Our enslavement to idols, to the gods of empires, continues. Of course Christians don't worship statues, but many are devoted to gods that still bear traces of the tyrant, the gods of the Israelites' captivity—gods that demand subservience, gods who enslave. I don't think the story of the Israelites wandering in the wilderness, learning to know God—is merely an item of biblical history. These are stories that help us understand what our lives are like with God. We still wander, we doubt, we wonder if it has been foolish to follow God, because we often find ourselves in the desert. The quail in the Bible are both a sign of God's extravagant care and a sign that the Israelites' desires need transforming. We are not exempt from the desert wanderings—but how else would we be transformed?

THE
VULCURE

UGLINESS
and BEAUTY

H A V E   Y O U   S E E N   T H E splendid fairy wren? The paradise tanager? I have tried to read the scientific explanations for their colors (fat-soluble...lipochrome pigments...black melanin seen through a keratin layer...optical interference...reflections based on regular periodic nanostructure of the barbules of the feather), but I am not convinced that *miraculous* is an unsuitable word. The Himalayan monal pheasant looks like an ancient Tibetan emperor wearing an elaborate cape of iridescent blues and greens and purples, with a yellow train and a sapphire crown. The great Victoria crowned pigeon looks like an elegant grandmother queen (or red-eyed alien) wearing a very fancy lacy hat. Birds are beautiful creatures.

I will probably only ever encounter some of these birds in books, but I have seen with my own bare eyes goldfinches drinking from the puddle in my driveway, bright orange orioles in my trees, bluebirds that perfectly match the sky flit by, and I am floored every time. You couldn't make up the peacock. If you were going to create a wonderland, of course you would put bright colors that fly into the sky. They are like abstract paintings that sing. And lay eggs. And it is all so beautiful and surprising: the blue and the yellow and the pink against the blue sky and the orange against the green grass—and then there is the vulture.

VOMIT AND EXCREMENT

New World vultures projectile-vomit into the face of anything that startles them. They eat excrement (especially human) and dead bodies. They defecate over their own legs. Most vultures are bald. This allows them to stick their entire heads inside a carcass without feathers to foul with blood and rotting flesh. A turkey vulture has very large and obvious nostrils. It is possible to see through from one side of its head to the other. This is not pretty. It is weird and scary. Vultures' heads are often disproportionately small compared to their bodies. This is not attractive. They sit hunched up with their heads sunk between their shoulders like a sulking teenager. They eat so much dead flesh at a meal that they are too heavy to fly, so they sit with their rough tongues in their mouths, hissing and grunting (they have no song), waiting to digest. A group of vultures isn't a flock; it's, much more ominously, a wake. Researchers going to band vulture chicks were so overcome by the unbearable smell of the nest that they lost consciousness (so I read on the Internet).

Most vultures have weak feet. Some have weak bills so that their meat must be partly rotted before they can tear it. You can always tell a turkey vulture from an eagle because the vulture wobbles in flight. It doesn't build a nest for its young—it leaves its eggs in crevices on the rocks. *Vulture* is from the Latin *vuellere,* meaning "to tear." Most people don't think of the vulture as a beautiful or noble creature. It is a long way from the splendid fairy wren. Its magic seems black, if anything.

"THY CARCASS SHALL BE MEAT"

I might be going out on a limb here, but I think the vulture's bad reputation has something to do with the fact that it eats dead bodies—that it would, in fact, be happy to eat *your* dead body—would fly around in circles if you were injured in the wilderness, waiting for you to die so that it could eat you. Proper burial was important to the Hebrew people. If you weren't properly buried, the vultures and other carrion eaters would tear your body up. "Thy carcass shall be meat" is a horrible thing to say to someone. It was one of the worst curses you could hurl in the biblical days. It was like wishing someone a fate worse than death.

In Deuteronomy God threatens the Israelites with this fate if they fail to abide by the covenant. Pestilence will cleave to them. God would smite them with mildew and ulcers and the scurvy and the itch, madness and blindness and confusion, and, worst of all, "Your dead body shall be food for all birds of the air." Goliath threatens David, "Come to me, and I will give your flesh to the birds." The prophet Hosea warns the unfaithful Israelites that they will be defeated by the Assyrian Empire. He says, "Set the trumpet to your lips, for a vulture is over the house of the LORD." In Revelation birds gorge on the flesh of the defeated "beast."

To be fair, vultures are not always specified in these passages, but they were plentiful in Israel and could be expected to show up if there was carrion to eat. As Jesus says, "Wherever the corpse is, there the vultures will gather." They appear in the text at moments of violence. They don't inspire sweet feelings of bird wonder. They are emblems of death and destruction in the Bible and beyond because they eat dead things. They don't actually participate in the killing. Death is not their fault, but they remind us of it.

People who profit from other people's suffering are called vultures. It is a word we use for the greedy, rapacious, and predatory. Vulture capitalists see a vulnerable business and swoop in to try to make a profit for themselves, usually at other people's expense.

Not one, but six supervillains in the Marvel Comics Universe are called "the Vulture." The vulture in the Looney Toons cartoons was stupid and slow. In *Babar the King,* where the various animals have trades that seem appropriate to the species, the vulture is a butcher. Shakespeare refers to the "vulture of sedition" and "the gnawing vulture of thy mind." I'm not sure exactly what he means, but it sounds familiar.

When Hazel, the elegant and charming mother of my friend Jennette, divulged her love for vultures, Kyle, a scholarly artist who is into Jung, said it must be a manifestation of her dark side. He didn't mean it as a negative thing. I've rarely known anyone who as readily embraces the dark side as Kyle—but still, most bird love would not strike anyone as dark. Vulture love may be an exception in our present cultural milieu. This, however, was not always the case. The line between what is ugly and what is beautiful moves around a lot over time.

NEKHBET

It might be hard for us to get our minds around, but there was a time when vultures had a reputation almost entirely different from the one they have now—a time when they were not tainted with darkness at all. Far from seeing vultures as representatives of death, the ancient Egyptians saw a great "mother god"—a huge, protective, high-flying goddess whose enormous wingspan could encompass and enfold everything. She was called Nekhbet. In some later texts of the *Book of the Dead,* Nekhbet is referred to as "Mother of Mothers who existed from the beginning, and gave birth to all that is."

Ancient Egyptians believed that the vulture existed only as female. This may have been because the vultures they were familiar with had no markings to differentiate the sexes. When the goddess bird wanted to reproduce, she merely opened her beak in flight and became impregnated by the wind.

This belief in the remarkably generative female vulture surfaces again in the medieval bestiaries, where the vulture is compared to the Virgin Mary. Vultures conceive without the seed of any male. So why should anyone scoff at the idea of a virgin birth? The *Aberdeen Bestiary* asks, "What can they say, those who are accustomed to ridiculing our priests when they hear that a virgin conceived?...They consider impossible for the Mother of God what is not denied as possible for vultures."

When we say "vulture" or read or see the word *vulture,* we think doom and gloom, but ancient Egyptians saw something else entirely. The vulture is a character in the ancient Egyptian hieroglyphic alphabet. It represents the sound that is used in the words *mother* and *grandmother.* See *vulture*; read "mother." That might blow a twenty-first-century Western mind, but vultures were not despised in antiquity.

NESHER

The Hebrew word *nesher* is often translated in our English versions of the Bible as "eagle," but most scholars agree that "griffon vulture" is at least an alternative, if not a more fitting translation. As vultures became more loathsome to us English speakers, translators couldn't quite bring themselves to use the word *vulture,* even if it seemed like the best choice—it wouldn't sound right to our Western ears. But when God says to Moses, "You have seen what I did to the Egyptians, and how I bore you on [*nesher's*] wings and brought you to myself," it's probably not an eagle to which God refers. This is an interesting twist.

> Like [a vulture] that stirs up its nest, that flutters over its young, spreading out its wings, catching them, bearing them on its pinions; the LORD alone did lead him.

> Bless the LORD, O my soul; and all that is within me, bless his holy name!...who forgives all your iniquity, who heals

all your diseases ... who crowns you with steadfast love and mercy, who satisfies you with good as long as you live so that your youth is renewed like the [vulture's].

Bestiaries claim vultures lived upward of one hundred years. It may be more like fifty, but they have long, vigorous lives.

Three things are too wonderful for me; four I do not understand: the way of [a vulture] in the sky, the way of a serpent on a rock, the way of a ship on the high seas, and the way of a man with a maiden.

They who wait for the LORD shall renew their strength, they shall mount up with wings like [vultures], they shall run and not be weary, they shall walk and not faint.

The eagle is a favorite emblem of empires. It's an excellent hunter and killer. Militaries the world over love to use it on their badges and banners. We've read these verses, imagining *that* bird, but what might it be like to be carried on the wings of a vulture, the great protective mother bird?

Vulture's wings are huge, but not powerful in the same way an eagle's are. Vultures fly higher than almost every other bird on earth, but not by their mighty personal strength as much as by (what I might call) a more communal energy. The sun warms the ground, which in turn warms the air. Often the sun warms the ground unevenly (for instance, when one side of a mountain is in the shade, while the other gets the full force of the sun). The warmer air expands, becoming less dense than the surrounding air mass—and the mass of light air rises. Many birds ride thermals (eagles included), but the vulture is like a thermal radical.

Most birds fly below five hundred feet. Vultures glide effortlessly on the winds at ten thousand feet. In 1973, a griffon vulture collided with a commercial airliner over Africa. It was flying at *37,900* feet! This is the highest altitude ever recorded for a bird. Their ability to fly that high isn't a result of exerting their own force—it isn't raw power and muscle that catapult the vulture upward. It is much more Zen than that. They open their wings and ride the currents. You can watch videos of this on ARKive.org if you are not lucky enough to be in a place that is frequented by vultures. The vultures look like they are flying in slow motion. They hardly flap their wings. All you hear is the wind and the occasional "flap." The way of a vulture in the sky is more Buddha than Thor. I think I might like that in a god.

Maybe God is a little bit more slow-motion than action-adventure—a patiently waiting sort of a God; a little quiet—behind the scenes. It takes a long time for people to get to know this God. People keep passing down their partial knowledge to successive generations, but still, we keep getting God a little wrong. After thousands of years, after Jesus Christ, we still haven't quite got Zeus out of our systems: power-hungry and petulant. God must be very patient—it is taking such a long time for our world to be transformed. Women are no longer viewed as property (at least not often). Slavery (though ever present) is not legal. We do not sacrifice virgins to the gods (at least not blatantly). I mostly believe we are in the process of being transformed (depending on the day and what is in the news), but it would take someone with an eternal and very far-seeing perspective, like a vulture at thirty-seven thousand feet, to trust the long view. Perhaps it takes a God with all the time in the world to trust this process—the slow, non-violent revolution—to see that some good might yet come amid all the setbacks and tragedy.

WITH WINGS LIKE A TURKEY VULTURE

I wrote an essay in 1994 where I reflected on Isaiah 40:31: "They who wait for the LORD shall renew their strength, they shall mount up with wings like eagles." I mentioned that I had been waiting for the Lord quite a long time but had not really felt much like I had been mounting up with wings like an eagle. I had been noticing the turkey vultures all around Jim's grandma's farm—how wobbly they were. This seemed more like my experience, waiting for the Lord—not mounting up but circling and tottering. Faith for me is not like the strong, smooth, sure-of-itself eagle soaring; but rather the waiting, wobbly, awkward circling of those-blown-by-the-merest-whiffs-of-wind turkey vultures. I mentioned that my faith journey didn't seem to involve some linear sort of advancing, but might better be described as swaying, rolling, and being blown. I said, "Progress of the soaring eagle variety doesn't apply to my experience so far."

I nearly fell off my chair when I discovered *nesher* could be translated as "vulture." Isaiah may actually have meant to say that those who wait shall mount up with wings like vultures—*not* eagles. Faith is more like circling than seizing. It is being lifted by thermals more than flying by the power of our individual wings.

We've formed some ideas of God and faith with the eagle in mind. The vulture God might give us a different perspective. Whether we are reading Scripture as first-century Jews or as twenty-first-century Christians, the Word seems to have the sort of life that continually startles. People may have been reading it carefully for thousands of years but this doesn't mean something new might not walk out of it. Isaiah points to a messiah (a savior) who "possessed no splendid form for us to see, no desirable appearance." In the Gospels we encounter a God who comes and dies. If we hope to hear the word of God in the Scripture, it might be good to listen as though we don't already always know what it's going to say—ready to be surprised by vultures, pigeons, a Savior who offers himself as food.

James Alison says, "A considerable part of the effect of the Christian revelation will be a shaking up of what is apparently 'right' and what is apparently 'wrong' as we get used to how falsified our 'reason' has been by our violence, how dangerous our 'goodness' is, and how long and slow is the path by which we enter into our right minds." If the Bible is not shaking us up, even blowing our minds, we may need to listen at a different frequency, dig deeper, read between the lines, open our eyes wider, hit it with a hammer, throw it out the window, dust it off and try again.

BLOWING MY MIND

When I started looking around, I realized pretty quickly that my ideas about vultures were extremely narrow—confined by my limited experience. When I think *vulture* I think *turkey vulture* because I'm from Minnesota and that's what I know. But there's a breathtaking range of vultures across the world. There are seven species of New World vultures and fifteen species of Old World vultures.

The king vulture is very striking. *Doom, gloom,* and *ugly* would hardly be appropriate words for it. It's face looks like a Picasso—some primitivist art; bright yellow, orange, purple, and red swatches of color outlined in vivid black—all angular lines and primary colors. Its eyes are concentric circles: black in the middle, surrounded by bright white, outlined by a vivid red. It is a New World vulture found in Central and South America. The Mayans revered it. It appears frequently in their ancient codices and hieroglyphics. Its blood and feathers were used to cure diseases.

Then there is the lammergeier. Even the name seems graceful to me. The lammergeier is more conventionally handsome than some vultures—it's not bald (this might help). It has interesting facial markings; a little curlicue of black lifting from the eye, like a ballerina painted for a dance or the kohl painted on the eye of an Indian bride. It's also well proportioned. Its head is not so small; its shoulders not so sulky. It lives only in mountainous terrain. (I'm going to report the facts and they might not seem pretty, but if you watched it flying, you might think so.) The lammergeier actually derives most of its diet from the marrow of bones. If the bones are small enough, it just eats them outright, but if they are large, the lammergeier drops them onto rocks to break them. It often has favorite rocks that it returns to again and again. The lammergeier was once known as the ossifrage—bone smasher (*frage* as in fragile). I find this strangely, beautiful—like it is somehow intimately acquainted with death, and with the marrow of life, and yet takes it lightly. In Iranian mythology the lammergeier is the symbol of good luck and happiness.

The Egyptian vulture is known for its intelligence. It breaks eggs with its beak and eats them, but if the eggs are large (like enormous ostrich eggs), it employs tools—takes stones and throws them at the egg to break them. It has a yellow face.

Have you seen the California condor? Resurrected from extinction, it's the largest flying bird in North America. It looks like a flapper of the roaring twenties with its frill of black neck feathers—like a sinewy boa.

The lappet-faced vulture, the largest vulture in Africa, looks like it's wearing some avant-garde designer coat: fuzzy white feathers on the chest accented by dramatic black feathers protruding in every direction. There is the white-backed, the white-headed, the palm-nut, and the hooded vulture. They are all unique and strange. *Miraculous* might be a suitable word.

I am thrilled when we find black vultures on the beach in Mexico on our winter break. The first morning we go out, there is one perched in the palm tree next to the pool. I feel like this is a gift. The vultures circle and land continually to eat the dead fish that have washed up from the sea. I am surprised when I watch a family who is visibly revolted by their presence (I forget that they are loathsome). The tips of the black vulture's wings are white. When they come in for a landing these tips look dainty to me, like a woman with a white-gloved hand giving a little wave. This is all a bit of a turnaround for me.

DEATH EATERS

Whatever surprising beauty you begin to find in the vulture's flying or markings or mythological history, the picture of a group of them tearing at a bloody corpse may send you reeling back to your initial revulsion. It is hard not to feel repulsed when you watch something eating a dead carcass. But of course, we are a species that eats dead meat, too—often meat that has been raised inhumanely on factory farms. The vulture, unlike us, rarely ever hurts a living thing. Most creatures have to kill to eat, but not vultures. With rare exceptions, their food has either died by natural causes or been killed by some other creature.

Instead of feeling repulsed by the eating habits of vultures, we might be grateful. Vultures take care of rotting remains that could otherwise spread diseases. They have uniquely strong digestive juices that kill bacteria and nasty pathogens. We may not be attracted to creatures that urinate on their feet, but this completely sterile fluid serves to cleanse them. They are remarkable purifying machines.

The Mayans referred to the vultures as death eaters. This struck them as a good, godlike thing because, after all, we need something to eat death (to digest it and rid it of its toxicity). Vultures stare death in the face and fear it not at all. It goes through their bodies and comes out harmless. They cleanse the world.

Vultures used to be plentiful in India, Nepal, and Pakistan. Their rapid decline in the last decade has made it clear how important they were to the health of the whole. A painkiller (diclofenac) fed to livestock turned out to be poison to the vultures that feed on their car-casses. Tens of millions of vultures have died from kidney failure brought on by the drug. The government of India recognized the havoc the loss of the vulture was wreaking: festering cattle harboring anthrax, surges of rabies due to an increase in the populations of feral dogs who were thriving without vultures to compete for food sources, the spread of harmful diseases. So they banned the drug to save the vulture. In an even more concerted effort, conservation groups and government agencies have opened "vulture restaurants" to provide safe meat for the birds to eat: local farm-raised meat without chemicals. Thriving vulture restaurants in South Africa, India, Nepal, and Pakistan host these loathsome, gloomy, godlike beasts.

The turkey vulture is also known as the *Cathartes aura,* which is derived from the Greek *katharsis,* meaning "to purify"; and the Latin *aureus,* meaning "golden": "the golden purifier." Maybe God is something like that—not so much like an eagle— not a fierce warrior god swooping in for the rescue or the kill, but a God who can take everything in and make it clean—a God who can make even death nontoxic.

JHATOR: THY CARCASS SHALL BE GIFT

The ancient Hebrews thought having your body eaten by vultures was a fate worse than death. "Thy carcass shall be meat" was one of the worst things you could say to somebody. Calling down the vultures was a terrible curse. But there are cultures where this is not at all the case. In Tibet, where the ground is rocky and the firewood scarce, burying and burning bodies has never been much of an option. The Buddhists there practice *jhator,* which means "alms to the birds," also known as sky burial. The monks chant mantras, incense is burned, and finally the bodies are laid out ceremoniously to be eaten by vultures. This is not seen as a bad thing at all, but rather the last act of generosity—in death, one provides food to sustain the living beings. It's an act of compassion and detachment from self.

It is difficult sometimes to see something from an angle that we are not used to, but it seems to me that love, generosity, the well-being of our life together on the planet rests on the possibility that we might do so.

WHAT IS BEAUTIFUL

The American commercial culture that runs through our veins tends to have a narrow definition of what is beautiful (to put it mildly). I don't think this is good for our psyches or our children or the earth. We need to do better than reproducing the stereotypical discourse. We desperately need to see beauty in places other than where we've been preprogrammed to see it. We need to expand the prescribed definitions, see outside the constricting, life-sucking limits. We need to see what is lovely in what the world has declared ugly or loathsome. Of course I love the paradise tanager, but there's something more rewarding about discovering beauty where I hadn't seen it before. To see beauty in new places, you don't have to trick yourself—you just dig around a little bit, pay closer attention, allow yourself to be opened.

We are often so caught up in our ability to make judgments that we deprive ourselves of a more lively imagination. What I judge is often a projection of my fear—fear that I am something that is unlikable; fat, old, weird, partisan, self-righteous, hateful. I am undoubtedly far more narrow-minded than I suspect. We are all going to die, whether old or young, and there will be pain in it. But what if we weren't smothered and dimmed and made mean by our fear? What if we could be attentive to what we encounter (the horny-casqued, the long-wattled birds, plants, people, buildings, feelings, pain, pleasure) and not be overcome with our assumptions about the goodness or badness, beauty or ugliness, but rather, be *interested* in them and curious about them? The narrow limits of our verdicts might be opened up. We need to have a little more imagination. The well-being of our children depends on this. I don't think I'm being dramatic here.

Olivia, my thirteen-year-old daughter, is reading *Bossypants* by Tina Fey. I didn't authorize this purchase on her Nook. I have completely lost control of her reading material, but I liked the passage that Olivia summoned me to hear her read. It was from a chapter where Tina Fey goes into how much more difficult everything has actually become for women. How it used to be that if you weren't blessed with a perfect body, you could just accept that and be interested in other things (books, maybe, or music or art or soccer). Now, if you are not hot, you are expected to make yourself hot through starvation, Pilates, or plastic surgery, if necessary. Olivia didn't think this was heading in the right direction.

Our determinations need constant reorientation. When labels start coming into our heads (loathsome, ugly, loser, winner), we should question them—recognize a label as the insubstantial thing it is, and let it go. It's not helpful. It's going to undermine our imaginations. Love something unusual. Kittens and lilies are fine, but maybe try the vulture or the dandelion, like Hazel, who fills her house with vulture paintings and poems. Hazel has a vulture sculpture in her yard. She dresses it in a red Santa hat at Christmas. She has these words tacked on the wall over her sink:

> Frowzy old saint, bald-
> headed and musty, scrawny-
> necked recluse on your pillar
> of blazing air which is not
> heaven; what do you make
> of death, which you do not
> cause, which you eat daily?
>
> I make life, which is a prayer.
> I make clean bones.
> I make gray zinc noise
> which to me is song,
> well, heart, out of all this
> carnage, could you do better?
> —Margaret Atwood

Sometimes we don't have great imaginations for beauty. Sometimes we don't have great imaginations for God. We are confined and limited by stereotypes and preconceived expectations. I believe that the word of God, far from confirming everything we already think we know, can surprise us. We are borne on vulture's wings.

THE

EAGLE

POWER *and*

VULNERABILITY

THE EAGLE HAS A MUCH better reputation than the vulture. It doesn't have a scrawny neck. It has traits that are more conventionally admired. The vulture eats death—the eagle defies it. The medieval bestiaries claimed that when an eagle got old and its wings got heavy and its eyes became clouded, it flew to the sun to burn off the mist from its eyes, then it hurtled itself down into a spring and submerged itself three times. It was immediately restored to all its glorious, youthful strength and beauty—no Botox or Pilates required. That's the kind of story people fantasize about. The eagle has been said to have the power, like the phoenix, to regenerate the wounded. If you could procure a tear from its eye, you could make yourself immune to death.

There's not a lot of bird-watching I can do sitting at my desk, looking out the window, but most days I see an eagle without even trying. We live near the river. My office is on the second floor. The window looks out over the hayfields and woods that surround the Rum River. There is a pair of bald eagles who have built a nest nearby. They stayed around the entire winter. This is unusual. Normally they leave when the river freezes over, but it's been a very warm winter. I like having them here, even though I'm sure it's a sign of climate change. They seem to have moved in permanently. However common-place it's become, I still feel a little excited almost every time I see them. If I am walking in the fields with my kids and I see one, or if we have guests for dinner and I see them through the kitchen window, I will always say (a little louder than necessary), "There's an eagle!" as if this is not just an everyday occurrence. I don't point out the crows or every other thing I encounter daily. I am not as excited to see my husband or the mail.

Eagles evoke some uncontrollable visceral response, in my experience, at almost any distance, but if you round the bend in the river and surprise one catching a fish fifteen feet in front of you, you will almost certainly feel *something*: blessed, or scared, or breathless. The bird emanates something that seems supernat-ural—practically mythic, like roc, or ziz, or the phoenix. They are giant birds with power. The legends of the great Native American thunderbird were based on the eagle. The thunder-bird, according to the legends, could easily take down a killer whale. It was the vigilant, intelligent, wrathful servant of the Great Spirit, and it was important that you go out of your way to avoid making it angry. It might shoot lightning bolts from its eyes, or flap its wings to make a terrible storm. When you

encounter an eagle, you are, in fact, encountering a large predator. If you are very close, it will probably make your heart pound.

If the vulture was seen as a mother-god figure, the eagle is
more like The Godfather. It's Zeus's bird, sometimes his weapon.
Zeus sent his eagle to eat Prometheus's liver as punishment for
his giving fire to humans. The liver would grow back. Zeus
would send the eagle to eat it again. Day after day this liver eating went on. Zeus took the form of an eagle to abduct
Ganymede, a beautiful young shepherd boy whom he made cup-
bearer of the gods. The abduction was not an offer that
Ganymede had the option to refuse. The eagle is the strongman,
all muscle and power. It represents brute force: we name our
weapons after it. The F-15 Eagle is among the most successful
modern fighter jets. The BAe Sea Eagle missile can take down a
ship the size of an aircraft carrier.

PATRIOTISM IS THE LAST REFUGE

I may respond viscerally to the giant living bird in front of
my eyes, but in some larger cultural/symbolic realm, I'm tired of
eagles. They do not move me when I see them on sports para-
phernalia, Harley T-shirts, biker tattoos, flags, bumper stickers,
bank advertisements, mortgage company logos, or billboards for
insurance companies. If I see any form of artwork that includes
an eagle (as one often does at rural art shows), I almost immediately dismiss the artist as somehow suspect or shallow. The eagle
is so hopelessly laden with cliché—massive power, fierce patriotism, killer instinct—it is getting a little old.

I loved being a part of my nephew's Eagle Scout ceremony. I liked writing the prayers for it and hearing the story of how he rescued a fellow Scout from the river. I appreciate the virtues the Eagle Scout demonstrates, especially that a Scout is helpful and kind. I love that the candidates organize and oversee a project to benefit the community, and I was so proud of Alex. But sitting next to men and boys amid a proliferation of eagle insignia on uniforms, I felt a little like an insurgent somehow—mutinous. What if the scoutmasters can smell the sparrow, the hen on me—a lack of patriotism?

I am afraid that governments and military systems sometimes take advantage of trustworthy, obedient, courageous, and kind young men, instilling in them a nationalism that is too narrow or one-sided and leads to wars these same young men fight and sometimes die in. I am thinking of how the spirit of God is like a dove, *not* like an eagle, thunderbird, or the F-15.

Alex is the farthest thing from an unthinking patriot. He is superthoughtful and smart, and the Boy Scouts have been wonderful for him. I'm just not crazy about the eagle's symbolic terrain. I am sitting in the Eagle Scout ceremony overthinking, as usual.

The eagle stands for courage and bravery. Courage and bravery seem like very important virtues. But I'm not sure what they mean in the abstract. I recently saw an ad on my home page: there was a picture of a dashing young investment banker saying, "I have guts, follow me." Guts for what, I want to ask—taking risks with other people's money? Aggressiveness and arrogance don't seem to me to be the same things as courage and bravery, but they often get confused in our culture.

The eagle is a symbol of loyalty, ferocity, and strength. Loyalty is good to a certain extent—but there are moments when rebellion is called for, a turning away. Strength serves a purpose—so does vulnerability. If we believe weakness is shameful, we are bound to marginalize or cast out the sick and the poor and the hungry. Power in itself is not something to celebrate, really, though this is not an opinion widely held. If it is something that propels the common good, advances equality, gives humans voice and agency—a power that allows us to concentrate or speak effectively—that is something to relish. But power is not neutral.

THE EAGLE AND EMPIRE

The eagle as a national symbol is not unique to the United States. It's used in the national heraldry of Albania, Armenia, Austria, Ghana, Iceland, Mexico, Moldova, Montenegro, Nigeria, Panama, Zambia, Yemen—to name but a few. The Babylonian, Assyrian, Roman, and Spanish Empires used the eagle as a symbol of their power. The Crusaders held it high as they conquered the "infidels." It was the imperial standard of Napoleon and an important symbol in the Third Reich. The Nazis called the day they were to invade Britain *Aldertag*, or "Eagle Day." The eagle means power wished for or exercised. Most nations seem to hope to have some eagle in the mix.

The bald eagle on the Great Seal of the United States of America holds a bundle of thirteen arrows in its left talon (referring to the thirteen original states) and an olive branch in its right talon. It is meant to symbolize that the United States of America has a strong desire for peace, but will always be ready for war. I wonder if being at the ready for war truly contributes very much to the prospect of peace. I am just thinking of how humans operate—couples, for instance, and parents and children. I have not found that always being ready for war helps me get along well with Jim. It is more likely to make me ready to attack him if he makes too much noise unwrapping his candy at the movie theater or if he drives what is in my opinion far too slow to get to church on time. In my experience, being ready for a fight undermines peace. (I realize this is the opposite of our national strategy.) I wonder what it would be like to have a robin on our national seal, or a chickadee.

When I mention I'm writing about the eagle, at least a dozen people tell me the story about Benjamin Franklin—how he objected to the eagle becoming the national symbol because he thought it was a bird of bad moral character, because it bullied smaller birds and stole their food. Benjamin Franklin thought the wild turkey would have been a better choice to represent our country. I wonder if it would have made any difference if we'd gone with that—if the body count would be lower. What if we admired what stays close to the ground and flies slowly and travels in flocks—something that eats berries and sports a wattle and a snood, instead of sharp talons? What if we chose something that "putts," "purrs," and "kee-kees" rather than something that flies fast and kills?

Eagles are not birds that look very friendly—with their furrowed brows and their dangerous-looking beaks. They look mean. Projecting an angry image doesn't seem like a great way to get along with the neighbors. It works better to offer them some brownies or a smile. This seems like very basic knowledge about how to get along. I would love to see a turkey on our national seal, on the lectern in front of the president when he speaks on national TV. It seems like everybody would have to act differently—less bravado, maybe, more naked or clumsy honesty—more foraging beneath the shady canopy, less like Zeus worshipers—more like turkey lovers.

EXCELLENT KILLER

The eagle is indeed an extraordinary killer. It has big leg muscles and powerful wings. These birds often start their lives as killers—newly hatched, right out of the shell—the older or stronger sibling in a nest kills the younger or weaker one. The parents accept this without protest.

Eagles have eyes the size of a human's and three times as powerful. They can see us far better than we can see them. They spot their prey from far away, sometimes more than a mile. They swoop in and power-dive. They are superfast. A golden eagle was clocked chasing a peregrine falcon at 120 mph.

The bald eagle likes fish. The golden eagle prefers rabbits, but eagles will kill most anything. The Philippine monkey-eating eagle kills and eats (obviously) monkeys—sometimes quite large ones. And sloths. The martial eagle, the largest eagle in Africa and one of the world's most powerful avian predators, eats cobras, pythons, green and black mambas, boomslangs, puff adders, storks, hares, hyraxes, mongooses, baboons, warthogs, antelope, impalas, goats, and lambs. Nomads in Kazakhstan train golden eagles to hunt for them. One bird named Alagym was reported to have killed fourteen wolves in *one* day. In the olden days of wolf killing, many human hunters would have considered that a good *year*. There are stories about eagles attacking planes—yes, planes. In the first days of aviation, the British Air Ministry provided official instructions on what to do if attacked by eagles. The French considered training eagles to attack enemy aircraft.

Ranchers and farmers from Africa to South Dakota have considered eagles a threat to their livestock. In fact, so much so that in the days before it was illegal (or in some cases even after it was), there were ranchers who instigated all-out war against them, poisoning them or employing helicopters or small planes, or hanging out of pickups to shoot at them with 12-gauge shotguns. As late as 1972, a pilot for the Buffalo Flying Service in Wyoming testified before a Senate subcommittee that ranchers had hired him to fly a chopper from which sharpshooters brought down more than five hundred eagles.

The eagles were not as much of a threat to the ranchers as they imagined them to be—their impact on livestock was minimal—but maybe it's just the kind of bird that inspires some sort of machismo rivalry. It brings out the fight, some sort of competitive instinct. Eagles are naturally better equipped to kill than are humans. They have beaks and talons that are strong enough to rip through flesh. We have fingernails and molars.

Eagles are especially good at what they do. They are big and fast and strong. They have excellent eyesight. That's cool. They are also killers. I wonder if making a stealth predator a national symbol is such a great idea. Big and fast and strong are not sustainable values. A lot of people seem to be with me on this and are moving toward small farms and slow food. People have started to build little eco-houses and trade their cars in for bikes. People are taking their money out of big banks and investing in local credit unions. Many people across the world are recognizing a need for a new paradigm if we hope to continue life on this earth—a paradigm that acknowledges the value of limits rather than pursuing unchecked power and expansion. How about adopting a slow bird with a sweet song for a new national direction?

THE BIRD IN THE BIBLE

Some of the most memorable places the eagle appears in the biblical text may have been mirages, as we saw in the last chapter. Though we have read "eagle" in English, "vulture" may have been a better translation for the Hebrew word *nesher*. The eagle isn't in the Bible as much as English speakers have supposed, but it has been the bird of Scripture that many have claimed to represent their faith. This seems just a little bit surprising to me, having explored and preached on the Gospels for the last twenty years. The eagle is rarely Jesus' go-to bird, yet it remains a popular cultural selection.

There are eagle Christian curriculums, schools, and how-to-be-an-eagle Christian sermons. There are eagle Christian evangelist agencies, eagle Christian colleges equipping people for their God-given destinies. Eagle Christians go forth fearlessly in the face of adversity and conquer their enemies.

I guess I can see why this sounds appealing. I memorized Isaiah 40:31 as a child—the one about those who wait upon the Lord rising up with wings like an eagle. Wings sounded freeing and adventurous. Eagle strength sounded good too. Superpowers in general seem to be perennially attractive to kids (mutant or god-given). If I had known the bird in the verse was a vulture, it might have changed the image of my desire, but I liked the idea of superpowers. It was the kind of strength that was valued in my culture. I was small. I was quiet. I liked to climb the tree at the edge of a farm field across from our house in the suburbs, and just sit there peacefully perched in the branches; but mounting up with wings like an eagle sounded like an interesting option.

Maybe the eagle is so appealing to us because the truth is— even as full-grown adults—we aren't really all that big (considering the scope of the universe and time). There is no superman. We are often weak and fearful and brokenhearted. Maybe the eagle is so appealing in part because it is difficult to be small and human and vulnerable. We start out in the world very tiny (usually less than ten pounds). And very weak (our bodies were floppy; if we tried to put one hand in our mouths, we often missed and poked an eye). We were little, helpless, weak babies. Erik Erikson, reflecting on human psychosocial development, says it's because we started out this way that "a sense of smallness forms a substratum in [our] minds ineradicably." And we are not very comfortable with our ineradicable smallness. We spend a lot of time trying to eradicate it.

That's on one end of our lives. On the other end is death. We aren't very comfortable with this either. In death, we will not only be small, but—we fear—nonexistent, or worse (or better, depending on how you think of it), food for worms. We hope our bodies will be resurrected or that our souls will go to heaven, but we know for sure that the bodies we have now will be food for worms or vultures or wild animals, or they will be ashes.

Our response to smallness, weakness, being out of control, vulnerability, eventual decomposing is usually not very accepting. We don't usually love what is small and weak and vulnerable in ourselves. Nor do we generally feel that loving toward what is small and weak and vulnerable in other adults. We feel threatened by our finitude and mortality.

When Adam and Eve were roaming around in the garden and suddenly saw they were naked and vulnerable, they hid from God. We are often ashamed of the need and vulnerability that are at the core of our humanness. We're afraid of being insignificant. We want to be big, and thus this becomes the sort of unquestioned assumption for the direction of human enterprise.

Maybe this trying-to-be-big was an important adaptation when there were large predators about, but the big animals are, sadly, mostly gone now. There are no more cave bears or cave lions waiting to eat us. There are hardly any tigers left. Perhaps it would be better for the world and our psyches if we could be a little more accepting of our vulnerability and our thoroughgoing interdependence. The Judeo-Christian Scripture seems pretty adamant, that God created us as we are and called it beautiful. Whatever our feelings may be about it, God, the Word indicates, loves us deeply as we are: naked and needy, dusty and mortal—beings with the remarkable ability to be conscious. Let's be as conscious as we can about our fears and desires and hopes and dreams.

The eagle-Christian combination is not just unhelpful, it's dangerous. When the Peterborough bestiary describes the lessons we can learn from the eagle, it compares the eagle's parenting to God the Father's. The father eagle, so it says, would expose his chicks to the sun,

> holding them in its claw in mid-air. If one of them steadily retains the bold gaze of its eyes, actively keeping watch in the glare of the sunlight, then that one is deemed to have vindicated its nature. However, any which turns away its eyes from the rays of the sun is rejected as being degenerate and unworthy of such a father; and nor is it considered worthy of rearing…[the father] does not condemn the chick from a cruel nature but from an impartial judgment and nor does it disown it like one of its own, but as if it were rejecting a stranger.

This does not sound like good news to me. It sounds like the writer took a bit of Christianity and mixed it with a medieval notion of what it takes to be a man, a good dose of stoic virtue, and a drop of brutality and callousness. It is a graceless sort of alchemy that still haunts us, I believe. The God in our Scripture is decidedly not an impartial judge who disowns the weak as if they were strangers—quite the contrary.

THE NATION

Every Fourth of July, there is patriotic fervor about, but I've noticed lately there is quite a lot of circumspection as well, with people looking at the many beautiful things about our country to be loved and appreciated and also acknowledging it has its faults—it's a mixed bag. It may be better than some places for certain reasons, and it may be worse than some places for other reasons.

The story of the nation of Israel as recorded in the Bible is different from the stories most nations try to tell about themselves. There are tales of heroes and battles won in the Bible—the Egyptians drown in the sea as the Israelites escape; Joshua fights the battle of Jericho; the people find a king who is "taller than any of the people." The eagle stories. But the narratives of triumph stand for about ten minutes before cracks start breaking through the surface. The Israelites escape Pharaoh as the moaning of Egyptian mothers who have lost their firstborn rises through the night. The stories are told in a way that invites questions.

The heroic narratives are sometimes so over the top that you wonder if they are meant as parody or farce. After David cuts off Goliath's head, he parades it through Jerusalem and brandishes it before King Saul so that "the whole world will know that there is a God on Israel's side." The women come out of all the cities of Israel, the text says, singing and dancing to meet King Saul, with timbrels, singing with joy, "Saul has killed his thousands, but David has killed his tens of thousands!" Saul gets petulant and jealous that they are attributing to David a greater body count.

It's grotesque, practically. It sounds so much like the dramas of a decadent monarchy that it's hard not to hear in the very telling a veiled critique.

The people clamor for a king. God doesn't like the idea—insists that a king will mean the loss of freedom. Institutions of leadership may arise in the text, but they are almost always undermined by counternarratives that expose their corruption.

David may be loved by God, but the people of Israel were first gathered around the commandments: do not kill; do not commit adultery. David commits adultery and then promptly has his lover's husband killed. Seeds for the undoing of the official narratives are always being planted. I like that in a book. I like that in a story of a nation. It gives the background, the real story to the life of a nation: the eagle, the vulture, and the sparrow.

The narratives of Joshua may sound triumphant, but in Judges, which comes right on its heels, the grandeur of the time is diminished by much more intimate stories of imperfect, vulnerable, and messed-up humanity: Samson and Delilah; the Levite whose concubine is raped by his fellow Israelites. In Judges the people of Israel start fighting among themselves, committing atrocities against one another. Almost immediately after the supposed conquest, snapshots of sorrow and defeat deflate the tale of glory.

In Leviticus there's a warning from God: don't behave abominably, "lest the land vomit you out, when you defile it, as it vomited out the nation that was before you." The book of Second Kings reports that once in Canaan, each generation of

Israel was worse than the last, and "GOD was furious with Israel." All the language of how Israel destroyed the Canaanites is used against itself in the Prophets.

For a nanosecond, the Israelites are heroes and conquerors, but then the story turns into a sort of slo-mo vomiting out: the people of the nation defile, and pollute, and mess up, and fail to love. They don't take care of the poor. The narrative of the nation of Israel may start out with a triumphant conquering, but it ends up with the land vomiting them out into Babylon.

As the testament of a nation, the Hebrew Scripture displays a remarkable capacity to be self-critical. It's one of the most interesting and wild and beautiful things about the Bible. It continually revises and unravels itself. There are many twists and turns. The seeds of the unraveling are planted even in what seem like the most straightforward stories.

JESUS AND THE NATION

A lot of people thought the Messiah would come to save the nation. Jesus is a bit of a surprise in this sense. He doesn't lead a crusade against the Roman Empire. He embodies a different approach to salvation.

Jesus says if anyone would be first, he must be last of all and servant of all. His disciples argue about who is the greatest, and Jesus takes a child and puts the child in the midst of them. He takes the child in his arms and he says, "Whoever receives one such child ... receives me; and whoever receives me, receives not me but him who sent me." He makes it sound like receiving God might be quite a bit different from receiving power as we are used to thinking of it.

Our nation says it desires peace—but then presents on its insignia a bald eagle—the fiercest bird. On the other hand, in the midst of a discussion about power, Jesus takes a child and says, "Here, embrace this."

Maybe we worship power, try our hardest to project strength and invulnerability, because we are afraid of something we don't need to be afraid of—something we would do better to embrace, like the vulnerability at the core of our humanness. Perhaps being open to this is precisely what makes peace and love and cooperation possible. It is this openness to vulnerability that allows us to receive God.

Our imaginations are limited by fantasies of power. The Incarnation is a story about a God who comes into the world as a naked, weak, little baby. It's a story that punctures narratives of a violent, all-powerful deity. It is about a God coming to disarm us by being utterly weaponless, absurdly vulnerable. God doesn't come in power to save us, according to the Christian narratives, but in weakness. I can believe this might work, because as far as I can tell, that's what love is like. It is something that slowly helps us realize that we have no need to protect ourselves. We don't need to defend ourselves. We don't have to hide who we are. We can be honest about everything. James Alison says, "Confession is the long slow process of being disarmed." In the light of God's radiant love, we can be at peace with ourselves and one another. I believe this revelation could change the world.

Maybe it's not by the *power* of God, by heroic conquering,

that people will be saved and set free, but by something much more vulnerable than that, something broken and shed. Not glory solidified, but power undone.

THE EAGLE REVISITED: RESURRECTION

In the 1960s, at the very time I was memorizing my eagle verse in Sunday school, hoping for some superpower, the eagle was showing itself to be vulnerable. The widespread use of DDT interfered with the bird's ability to process calcium—the eagle was starting to lay eggs that were catastrophically fragile. The shells would become so thin that they would break when the parents sat on them to keep them warm. Our national bird was becoming extinct. In Ben Franklin's day, there were hundreds of thousands of bald eagles in North America. By 1963 there were only 417 nesting pairs in all the Lower 48 states combined. The emblem of our nation's strength was becoming weak.

In 1962, the *New Yorker* began publishing segments of Rachel Carson's *Silent Spring*. For the first time, people across the country became aware of the cost of synthetic pesticides. We began to realize that petrochemicals were decimating the bald eagle and other bird populations. Carson wrote, "Over increasingly large areas of the United States, spring now comes unheralded by the return of birds, and the early mornings, once filled with the beauty of birdsong, are strangely silent." In *The Aeneid,* the pathway to hell is *Averno*—in Greek this means "a place without birds." The entrance to hell is a place without birds. People across the country seemed to know this intuitively. Carson's research caused the nation to wake up.

The public concern created by the dying birds was in many ways the beginning of the environmental movement in our country. The Environmental Defense Fund was formed in reaction to the DDT problem. The group enlisted scientific experts, ornithologists, ecologists, toxicologists, carcinogen experts, insect control specialists, and ordinary citizens everywhere to work together to get DDT banned and help save the birds. We did not revile the eagle for its emerging vulnerability. Instead, we came together as a nation to nurture it.

In 1967 the eagle was declared protected. In 1972 DDT was banned. In 1973 PCBs were banned in situations where they were likely to contaminate the environment at large. The national wildlife refuge system began to provide habitat for nesting pairs of bald eagles. Various centers throughout the country began to breed eagles in captivity and released them into the wild. By 1981, through the work of bird lovers and environmental laws, the bald eagle population in the Lower 48 had doubled. By 1993 there were 4,500 nesting pairs. By 1995 the threat was officially declared to be reduced. In 2007 the federal government officially removed the bald eagle from the endangered species list. These days they are everywhere. Though it is impossible to have an accurate count, some say there are more than nine thousand nesting pairs in the Lower 48—some say fifty to seventy thousand if you include Alaska and Canada. That is a lot of birds.

Maybe the eagle is a good national symbol after all. Not because of its capacity to do violence or fight. Not because it's such a good, strong killer, but because it shows how when we pulled together we helped bring something back from the brink of extinction. It turns out to be the symbol of what we can do when we work together—the resurrective value of cooperation. Maybe we can do this again.

We nurtured what was vulnerable as a nation and brought something beautiful to life again. I say, let's embrace the eagle as our symbol after all, to represent not our allegiance to power, but our commitment to hope. The resurrected eagle tells us we do not need to surrender to hopelessness. I literally see one every day.

6

THE OSTRICH

COMEDY *and* TRAGEDY

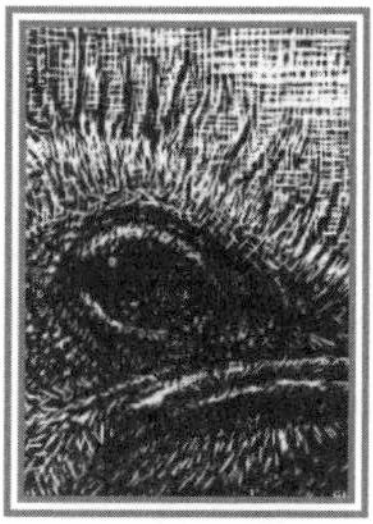

IT WAS SOMETIME IN THE mid-1990s. Jim and I were recently married, living in a chicken coop we'd converted into a living space on Jim's grandma's farm. We didn't have electricity or plumbing or jobs, but we had the most beautiful garden. At night we lay in bed and read Wendell Berry to each other, imagining we could resurrect the old farm in a small-scale sustainable way—live like the characters in his book. It seemed like a good thing to do with our lives. We had learned to tap maple trees and can salsa, red sauce, pickles, and jams. We dried ber-gamot and lemon balm and made our own tea bags to give as presents at Christmas. We spent a lot of our time creating papier-mâché boxes in which to present the tea bags. We became very focused on this, spending hours, *days,* sitting on the floor cutting and taping, papier-mâchéing, and painting. Jim painted cranes, seagulls, and fish. I did abstract designs. If we'd had cows that needed milking, they would have burst. We forgot to buy oil for our lamps. We were not very practical. We had degrees in painting and theology. We didn't really know how to be farmers, much less generate any income from it. Someone suggested we try ostriches.

In retrospect, it seems like it must have been some huckster-charlatan-get-rich-quick schemer; some bow tie–wearing, mustached, midway barker, but I think it might have been our friend Brett.

For a brief period in the nineties, some eager entrepreneurs believed that ostriches were poised to become the cows of the twenty-first-century. They took less land and effort to raise than other livestock. Their meat was red and delicious *and* low in fat. Ostriches could adapt to any sort of weather. They laid eggs big enough to feed a family of four. In fact, *every part of an ostrich could be sold for a great profit,* the pyramid schemers exclaimed. Texans were clamoring for ostrich-hide cowboy boots. You could sell the beaks and the toenails to the Japanese, who ground them up to make aphrodisiacs. The feathers went for $200 a bird.

You might have to pay tens of thousands of dollars for a nesting pair, but you could make the money back in no time. I don't think Brett was really giving us the pitch as much as passing along stories he had heard—some people said you could get very rich very quick by farming ostriches.

Jim and I don't do many things quickly. It takes us months to decide what sort of shade to buy for our bedroom window, and then several more to get around to doing it. I'm talking a bedroom window treatment. We generally do not move fast on things, and we don't make big purchases. In twenty years of marriage, we never spent more than $5,000 on a car. We built our own smallish eco-home after we moved out of the chicken coop. We would not even remotely consider spending $50,000 on a pair of giant flightless birds.

It also didn't seem like the kind of sustainable practice we were looking for—raising African birds in Minnesota and then cutting them up into pieces to sell to people in Japan and Texas. We have not yet managed to slaughter a chicken. I could not imagine us trying to butcher an ostrich. The whole enterprise seemed slightly absurd. And so it was. Grandparents in Florida and Texas spent their retirement money on pairs that simply didn't breed. Couples that did reproduce often had chicks that were fragile and required expensive veterinary services. Ostrich sandwiches, ostrich liver pâté, ostrich tenderloins never became the new American meat. Low fat is passé. Chefs are serving up grass-fed beef, goat headcheese, duck heart ragu, and pickled pig's feet. I have seen every sort of native meat on menus lately, but ostrich, never once. Many people who invested in the brief ostrich-farming craze were left to kick around in the dust with their nearly worthless birds. We didn't turn out to be farmers. Jim got work building timber-frame homes. I started a church. We do live with our friends on a "farm," but we all drive somewhere else to work. We still read Wendell Berry.

A COMPANION OF OSTRICHES

An ostrich is a strange bird. It's enormous: six to nine feet tall, weighing as much as 350 pounds. It has prehistoric-looking hooflike feet with only two toes. There is a big black claw that protrudes from one of the toes. It curls like the fingernail of a fairy-tale witch. An ostrich has spindly legs that look like sticks until you get to the thighs, which look strangely human—like an Olympic runner's. Then, bang, this big wide body puffs out drenched in sinuous feathers. Out of the bulging middle rises the snakelike neck that can twist and bend and swivel. Finally, there's the tiny head with massive eyes: two inches in diameter, the largest of any land vertebrate—about the size of a billiard ball. The ostrich whistles, snorts, and grunts, as well as making a sound that's like the roar of a lion. Aristotle concluded that it was neither bird nor beast, but some peculiar mixture—a giant avian creature with wings that couldn't fly.

In the Bible, Job laments that he used to be important, wealthy, and respected, but then he lost everything. Now, he says, "I have become like dust and ashes...a brother of jackals, and a companion of ostriches." This may be meant to be a purely tragic image, but there is something about it—something around the edges, that seems a little bit funny. Think of the ostrich. Think of Job hanging with the ostrich. I really don't mean to be insensitive.

My friend Abigail Pelham—who is a brilliant, original, and remarkably funny (yes, funny) biblical scholar—suggests that although Job is most often seen as a tragedy, it is possible to read the book as comedy. Abby says, "It is not his physical suffering or his personal losses that are the worst of Job's predicament" in Job's opinion, "but the fact that his suffering and loss have toppled him from his former position as the central figure of the world in which he lived."

When Job says he has become like a companion of ostriches, it is in the midst of a lengthy complaint where he explains his former greatness in detail. Job used to be great and people thought he was great—one of the greatest men ever. In fact, he was so much greater than most people that when he walked through the streets, the crowds parted for him and fell into a hushed silence. "After my speech," Job remembers rapturously, "they didn't respond. My words fell gently on them; they waited for me as for rain, opened their mouth as for spring rain. I smiled on them; they couldn't believe it." Job claims his words were like rain to these people whom, he soon makes clear, he didn't have much respect for. He "disdained" their fathers too much "to set [them] with the dogs of [his] flock." He claims these people brayed like animals huddling together "under the nettles...a senseless, a disreputable brood." These people of no import deigned to taunt Job now and laugh at him.

We often feel so much sympathy for Job—the righteous, innocent man who has been treated unfairly, that we hardly notice he may be an unreliable narrator: his words were like rain to the huddled masses? Really? It's possible that Job overestimates his bigness, greatness, and centrality. People tend to do this. If we are central to the world, it is mostly through our own eyes. We can't really help this (being trapped a little in our own brains), but it's a little bit funny thinking of us all walking around this way, in separate bubbles—privately obsessed with ourselves.

We spend a lot of time and energy fearfully propping ourselves up in our own minds—making sure we have some case for being more righteous, or more *something*—more smart, more cool, more free, more powerful, more contemplative, more humble, more wise—almost anything will do—just *more* than other people. But it is a futile enterprise—not something really worth the time we spend engaging in it. But still we persist in this vain game, bouncing between despair and grandiosity. There is some incessant narcissism at the heart of the human condition that is a bit laughable. Abby says, "It is tragedy which proclaims the grandeur of humankind. Comedy tells us the grandeur is a sham."

When God finally arrives on the scene in Job speaking from the whirlwind, God directs the spotlight away from Job—away from humans pretty much entirely. "God's questions direct Job's attention out to the multiplicity of animals which inhabit the complex, diversely populated world." Job and his friends go on and on, trying to determine what and who is righteous, what is justice and injustice, who is moral and who is immoral; is Job innocent or is he guilty. God comes and changes the subject—shifts the focus to birds and beasts, storms, thunder, hoarfrost, and the sea—and spends no time evaluating their morality. God speaks admiringly of the diverse and complex life in the world without passing judgment on any of it. The horse is fast. Behemoth's strength is in his loins. The ostrich lacks wisdom, but God doesn't regard it poorly. The vulture's young ones suck up blood. God feeds them.

The effect of God's speeches is humbling. Job laments that he has become like a companion of ostriches. In God's speech, the ostrich comes across as a bit of a fool, flapping its wings all around as if it is proud of them, even though they are useless. God does not condemn the ostrich for its foolishness or for forgetting that a foot may crush its eggs or that a wild animal may trample them. God does not even condemn it for laboring in vain. But God does note that it lacks self-discernment. It is not very wise. It seems plausible to suggest that Job has similarly been lacking in self-discernment. Perhaps Job is spot-on when he says he has become like a companion to ostriches, but perhaps he always was.

For all our bluster and all our desire for grandiosity and significance, we are in fact animals: large-brained primates with a tragic-comic capacity for a sometimes overwrought self-consciousness. We spend so much time preening our wings, worrying about who we are—where we fit in a hierarchy—and so often this labor is in vain.

"Tragedy admires man. Comedy feels a little bit sorry for him." We think we are kings or queens, masters of the universe or at least our own destiny. We forget that a foot may crush us, or that the wind may knock us down. We are not in control. We may strive for elegance, but we are still subject to gas and sloughing skin and dirty pores. Most of our joints will eventually fail us. We have big brains with which we can imagine great things, but we can't *really* get off the ground. It's like we have wings but we can't fly. I mean, I know there are planes and rocket ships, but we can't escape mortality—we are made of blood and bone. We are (so far) creatures of the earth. We are bound to the ground.

Abby says, "It may be that the author [of Job] has written a comedy for the express purpose of exposing the tragedy that lies at the heart of human existence: the tragedy is that it is a comedy." She adds: "Although we (usually) do not laugh at Job," because we identify too closely with him, "there are characters in the book who do. The group of outcasts which Job calls 'a senseless, disreputable brood'... These people do not identify with Job in the least." The ones at the bottom find the once-greatest-man-in-the-world funny.

Maybe the tragedy would not be so heavy if we didn't hold quite as tightly to our dignity—if we were more readily able to laugh at ourselves—if we could see something of our hilarity: hiding our smells, marking our territory like dogs, buying millions of dollars' worth of skin cream, trying so hard to *be somebody* when we already are. Wrinkles are not tragic. We are funny beings.

FUNNY PEOPLE

The 1990s weren't the first time ostrich farming failed. But whereas in the nineties people were betting on the potential skyrocketing popularity of lean red meat, in the late 1800s it was all about the feathers. The middle class was becoming more prosperous, and people had a little more money to spend on nonessentials—like more and more lavish hats. Milliners outdid one another with elaborate displays of a wide array of fancy feathers—and not only feathers, sometimes whole bodies of birds—not ostriches, obviously, but snowy egrets, blackbirds, and the heads of pigeons were quite popular. Frank Chapman, a noted ornithologist concerned with how this trend was impacting bird populations, took a bird count one day as he walked through Manhattan. He counted forty varieties of native bird species including meadowlarks, warblers, and owls, that had been killed, plucked, disassembled, or wired up on most of the seven hundred women's hats he saw. Ostrich feathers were especially popular. At one point they were worth almost as much per pound as diamonds.

Because ostriches don't fly, their feathers are unique. They don't have the tiny hooks that lock together the strands of most bird feathers. So instead of being smooth and sleek, they are light and fluffy. They flutter sensuously—reflecting light and registering even the smallest breath of air. They were used on dress collars and in feather boas as well as hats—they feel good brushing against your face.

Ostrich feathers were also used in feather dusters and fans. They even had a place in the church's liturgy. The "flabella" were fans of ostrich plumes tipped with peacock feathers. They were waved over the consecrated body and blood of Christ. This practice was derived from the days when fans were waved over dead animal sacrifices to keep the insects away. The famous "papal flabella" were mounted on long poles and carried by chamberlains who waved them over the pope when he was carried to and from the altar or audience chamber on his processional chair. The ostrich feathers became a mark of honor for church dignitaries. I hear they are also quite popular as sex toys.

The demand for ostrich feathers was so great in the 1880s that ostriches were nearly hunted to extinction until some enterprising folks decided to start farming them. In the 1850s ostrich farms began to spring up in South Africa and Australia. At first it went great and some farmers became wealthy. In Oudtshoorn, South Africa, the feather farmers displayed their wealth by building

"Ostrich Feather Palaces." When I first heard this term I imagined (irrationally) some sort of fairy-tale castle made of feathers—some sort of feathery nest with soft walls and floors of down. I was disappointed to find that they were actually just lavish homes built with the money made during the feather boom era.

When World War I broke out, the feather market collapsed. Huge frivolous hats went out of fashion. Ostrich feather farmers, thrown into financial ruin, began shooting their flocks, which were no longer worth the price of their feed. Tens of thousands of birds were gunned down (I swear I read somewhere) with machine guns. It is tragic and comic: women with birds on their heads, the price of a feather, once-wealthy farmers with fields full of animals that are now useless to them.

STUPID BIRDS

The attempt to get rich quick off ostriches has not been a very successful endeavor. The accounts of farmers who lost out in the most recent ostrich-farming craze often sound bitter and frustrated. Their frustration manifests toward the birds more than toward their own susceptibility to questionable schemes. Many of these farmers go on and on about how stupid ostriches are, seemingly unaware that their own judgment is implicated.

They complain that the birds are so moronic they don't know when to stop eating. They bemoan the males that would go into "frenzies" during breeding time. If there was a hole in the fence, one farmer reported, the birds would try to walk through it, even if it meant ripping off their own heads.

The one fact everyone seems to know about an ostrich is that it sticks its head in the sand. It's the bird's most famous characteristic and an image we use frequently to characterize people who refuse to face the truth about something. It might be true that people stick their heads in the sand, but actually, ostriches don't.

The myth that ostriches stick their heads in the sand may have come in part from Pliny's *Natural History,* written in the first century. He claims that ostriches "imagine, when they have thrust their head and neck into a bush, that the whole of their body is concealed." Pliny's work is amazing (if given at times to crazy remedies). His *Natural History* is one of the largest single works to have survived from the Roman Empire to the modern day. He tries to cover the entire field of ancient knowledge. Later encyclopedias were modeled on his work. But Pliny was wrong about the ostrich.

The ostrich passage in Job, a far more ancient text than Pliny's, didn't do much for the ostrich's reputation either. It says the ostrich is cruel to its young and that "God has made her forget wisdom, and given her no share in understanding." It's possible the poet meant to reflect on a human sort of foolishness, but this isn't what most people take away from the text.

I have a used copy of Alice Parmelee's *Birds of the Bible* written in the fifties. It once belonged to the Beth-Eden Baptist Church Library. Parmelee observes that the book of Job is not entirely correct about the ostrich. She says the ostrich does not, in fact, deal cruelly with its young. Though I haven't found a single other marking in the book, someone has circled this line in pencil and scrawled in the margin (in what looks to me to be church-lady handwriting), "This statement is wrong. The Bible is true." Clearly the ostrich is stupid. It says so in the Bible.

ALIEN INTELLIGENCE

Ostriches don't treat their young like humans do. They aren't mammals. They can't feed their children at their breasts. They don't have any. The size of the gray matter in their heads is smaller than the size of the matter in ours, but the ostrich has survived as a flightless bird on a continent with every imaginable predator and competitor for 120 million years. We have been around less than the merest fraction of that. In some ways we hardly seem in a place to judge.

Many scientists argue that intelligence may be more complicated than we once believed—harder to define across species. Some say plants could be called intelligent because they can sense their environment and adjust their morphology, physiology, and phenotype accordingly. This is not exactly something we can do. Some biologists believe octopuses and squid and other cephalopods are examples of advanced cognitive evolution, though it is hard to tell what's up with them because they are so fundamentally different from us—their nervous system is entirely "other."

Many of the flightless birds known to humans evolved on islands. It takes a lot of energy to fly, and if you are on an island and there are no large predators about, it makes evolutionary sense to adjust to a different lifestyle: on the ground or in the water. Gigantism is also something that often evolves on islands. In the absence of large mammalian carnivores, the ecological niches for large predators may be occupied by birds, reptiles, or rodents, which grow to huge sizes compared to mainland relatives. Tenerife giant rats, Madagascar's hissing cockroach, Galápagos turtles, and King Kong are all examples of island gigantism.

Cuba had a giant flightless owl. Mauritius had the dodo. New Zealand had thirteen or more species of giant flightless birds. There was once what was called the elephant bird, a ratite like the ostrich. It was absolutely enormous—10 feet tall and 880 pounds. Remains of their fossilized eggs have been found. They have a circumference of more than three feet.

Most of these gigantic flightless birds didn't survive the advent of humans. People probably hunted the giant elephant bird to extinction, or ate too many of its eggs. Humans brought diseases with them to islands and cats and dogs.

The ostrich is truly a rarity in the face of all this. It is huge, it is flightless, and it is not extinct. It survives in Africa, an enormous continent with fierce predators, lions and jackals and hyenas and people. And not only predators but enormous herds of competitors for food. It lives in large open spaces with no place to hide. The behavior of an ostrich is highly evolved and extraordinarily refined for its circumstances. It is faster than any other animal on two legs. I watched a film from the Discovery Channel where they were clocking the speed of an ostrich on a treadmill. The scientist mentioned that its legs are similar to those of the *Tyrannosaurus rex,* but the ostrich is faster. It can outrun most of its predators, maintaining speeds of forty-four miles per hour for up to thirty minutes. People (doing the sorts of things people do) have been known to put saddles on them and race them.

The fact that they can be frustrating to people who try to farm them might have to do with the fact that in the wild they are nomads with harems. Trying to get them to live inside fences, and to mate as we think they should, might drive both the farmed and the farmer a little insane. Maybe it is not stupidity that drives them to walk through the hole in the fence even if it rips their own heads off—maybe it's something like desperation. They are born to run, roam, and mate promiscuously.

Ostriches live and travel in groups of five to fifty birds. There is usually one male in the group who mates with various females, but it forms a pair bond with only one, who becomes the major (alpha) female. She is the one who leads the nomadic pack.

Males sometimes fight one another to establish their spot with the ladies. They slam their heads into each other with great force. This may be what farmers complain of as "frenzy." But after the frenzy, the actual mating dance is quite lovely. The male performs for the female, opening his feathers and beating his wings. He bows before her, and if he sufficiently impresses her, they start grazing together until their movements are synchronized. Eventually the grazing becomes secondary to the dance. The male then excitedly flaps his wings as the female circles around him. He scratches into the dirt—symbolically clearing out a nest in the soil. He winds his head in a spiral motion, she drops to the ground and he mounts her. It is like some ancient native magic dance. I have seen human mating rituals that are far more crude.

Sometimes lone males join the group during mating season, providing more partners for the females. Eventually all the females lay their eggs in one big group nest of about twenty eggs, which the main pair take turns incubating. The major female somehow knows which eggs belong to her, and she makes sure these stay in the middle of the communal nest, but both she and the male are careful to cover as many eggs as possible. The outlier females might mate with other males from other groups and leave eggs in other nests as well. It is not the sort of lifestyle humans generally advocate—but it is a very good strategy for ostriches; one might even call it brilliant.

The female sits on the eggs during the day because her colors match the sand. The male sits on them at night, because he is black and blends into the darkness. If a predator detects this clever camouflage technique and comes near, the mother or the father, rather than staying seated on the nest, will run from the nest to try to distract the predator. Although the poetry in Job makes it sound like the parents are unconcerned with their eggs, leaving them carelessly on the ground, this behavior is not a lack of concern but rather a diversionary tactic—like trying to divert the enemy by drawing the fire away. (You could think of it as more brave than stupid, really.) The eggs stand a better chance of staying camouflaged if the parent is not sitting on them. Once the chicks hatch, no preference is shown for whose is whose. The major couple raise all the babies with great care.

Sidi Mohamed (sometimes referred to as the "ostrich-boy") told the story of how he wandered off from his parents in 1945 in South Africa when he was five and found an ostrich nest where chicks were hatching. The ostrich parents took such good care of him that he allegedly stayed with them for ten years. He said that at night his ostrich parents sheltered him with their wings. Finally he was caught by mounted ostrich hunters and restored to his real parents, who presumably made him live in a house and eat people food. Ostrich wings are not good for flying, but they make good shelters for chicks, even little boys if we are to believe Sidi Mohamed. The parents use their wings like large umbrellas to create shade for the babies or to protect them from rain.

The communal life works well for the ostrich. It is a good strategy for defense. Their huge eyes and long necks help them to see great distances and they watch out for one another. When ostriches sense the presence of hunters that they can't escape by running, they lay down in the sand. This is probably the behavior that led to Pliny's misobservation and the myth about the head burying. But it's actually a pretty smart trick. The ostrich's sandy-colored neck and head are camouflaged in the sand. It holds its wings and tail low so that the heat haze of the hot dry air makes it appear as a nondescript lump. It looks like a bush or a pile of dirt rather than food.

Ostriches don't have large brains like ours. They can't write books or build factories or make bombs. If an intelligence is alien to us, maybe we don't readily recognize it, but this may speak more to our own lack of perspective, our own limited way of seeing, the arrogance of our species, than it does to some objective assessment. Ostriches may look silly, but there they are—grazing alongside zebras, gazelles, giraffes, and elephants, peacefully sharing what little resources the desert provides.

MA'AT

The ancient Egyptians are always good for a different perspective. There was a time before Job, and before Pliny, when the ostrich actually enjoyed a great deal of respect. In Egypt, the ostrich feather was the hieroglyph for truth and justice. It was the symbol for the goddess Ma'at, who embodied balance. She wore an ostrich feather in her crown. When they died, ancient Egyptians believed they were taken to the Hall of Ma'at, where their hearts were weighed against her ostrich feather. If one's heart (or conscience) was heavier than the feather (because he or she had failed to live a balanced life), the heart was thrown into a lake of fire. If the heart was light, on the other hand, it meant the person was free to join Osiris in the underworld. It was balance and light-heartedness that led to freedom. This sounds about right to me.

LOVER MOTHER

In the creation account in the book of Genesis, God speaks and divides and orders. God makes all the wild animals, and then God makes man to look after them. The human plays a central role. His part is key: he names the animals, none of which suffice for companions, so God makes another human. Of course this doesn't end up going all that well. The couple desire to be like

God. There is some blaming and shame. The couple's first son kills the second. All this takes place in the first few pages of the Bible.

When God speaks of creation in Job, the images have a different feel. God comes in a *whirlwind* and asks Job, "Where were you, little man, when I birthed the world?" The images are not of God ordering chaos, but of God giving birth to life: weird, beautiful, diverse life; and God really focuses on the weird and the wild life: ostriches, vultures, goats, and the sea. In Job, the sea bursts forth from God's womb. God doesn't defeat Leviathan, the sea monster of chaos who breathes fire; or Behemoth, the land monster whose bones are tubes of bronze. God speaks adoringly for quite a long time about Leviathan's chest and feet and skin and teeth—and about Behemoth's belly and bones and mouth.

The whirlwind doesn't speak of subduing, censoring, or putting man in charge. God marvels—marvels at the wild beasts at play and the snorting horses whose rage swallows the ground. The sea is the archetypal symbol of the forces that threaten humanity. In this poem God makes garments for it, swaddles it like a baby. God goes on and on about all the wild life as though God loves it—all of it.

Sometimes people read this poem as if it is meant to demonstrate God's omniscience and omnipotence—as if the point was for God to draw all eyes to Godself and all God's greatness. But God really isn't praising Godself as much as adoring what God gave birth to—like a mother admiring her children more than a patriarch demanding subservience and worship.

God does not speak gloriously of the animals because they are all focusing on God or because they have made God the center of their lives. God just seems to *like* them—to be enamored of them, whether or not they are paying any attention to God.

This is a very different sort of stance than Job, the once-greatest-man-who-ever-lived, takes. Everyone's eyes used to be on him. The crowd parted when he walked through it. Job disdains the pathetic lives of the "unruly brood" who are like animals to him. His fall from greatness is his great tragedy.

God more or less ignores Job's great drama in this particular bit of poetry—or perhaps models a different way of being. God speaks passionately about the unruly brood—God sets the wild asses free. God sends rain to the land that is uninhabited by humans. The uninhabited land can hardly be said to respect or worship God, and yet God satisfies "the waste and desolate land" and causes it to sprout vegetation.

When God comes in and takes the focus off Job and Job's tragedy, it could seem as though God is being unkind or inconsiderate. Like the humans were claiming more importance for themselves than what was really warranted and God is frustrated by this, maybe a little punitive and snarky.

But maybe it is more of a graceful move—a great gift. Maybe God is saying, "Look, stop focusing on yourself, look around for a minute—look at it all. It's all so beautiful and mysterious and complex—and bigger than you, way bigger than you. Consider the birds, man. Stop being so consumed with yourself, so anthropocentric." Maybe it is not meant to diminish us in some scornful way, but rather to diminish us in a way that sets us free. God is trying to give us a break—consider what is not you, what is beyond you. Stop posting your every move on Facebook—go outside for heaven's sake.

We are large-brained mammals. Cool. We grow old and we die. We may not be into that, but maybe it's not exactly a tragedy. We do things other animals can't—but check out the sea, man. We call the ostrich stupid—but what are we thinking—the birds have been around far longer than we have. It seems a bit presumptuous to mock their bird brains.

Abby says that God has shown Job "a world different from anything he could have conceived: terrible in its nonanthropocentricity, but, nevertheless, wildly beautiful and madly loved." We are not the gods of the earth. We may be frustrated that we do not get all of the creator's attention, but we *need* a God like this—the world does, in order to survive: a God who cares for all of creation, not just humanity. We are in great need of a God who loves the wilderness, the wild, who gives rain to the places humans can't even touch. "Whereas the world of Job and his friends is cramped and narrow," Abby says,

> God's world is wild and beautiful.... [God] shows [Job and his friends] what the world is like, and what he shows them is so much better than what they have come up with on their own. "Here is where you really live," God tells Job. "You do not live in that narrow world you thought you occupied. That's not real. That's something you made up. Come out here and be free, as you were meant to be."

Maybe we have identified so much with Job's tragedy because we often find it difficult to have a larger view. God does not come across as uncaring in this poetry so much as widely car-ing—caring in some way that is beyond our ability to conceive.

The ostrich is foolish, forgetful, lacking in wisdom, overly proud of its wings that can't fly. But God doesn't condemn the ostrich for its behavior. God loves all God's crazy animals. The ostrich flaps its flightless wings with joy, and "when she rouses herself to flee, she laughs at the horse and his rider." The ostrich laughs at us. Maybe it is just the sort of companion we need.

God is not judging, censoring, or slaying any part of the wild creation in this poetry—God gave birth to it, and like a mother, God is nursing it, swaddling it, and seeing to its upbringing. It may be a long process, but God is loving the world into fully being.

T H E
SPARROW

CONTEMPT *and* COMPASSION

IN THREE SHORT verses Jesus both acknowledges that sparrows are (nearly) worthless to humans and that not one of them is forgotten by God. He uses this to say, "Don't be afraid, don't be anxious; of course God cares for you. Every hair on your head is numbered." If God in Job seemed a little put off by some human tendency to self-importance, here Jesus wants to emphasize that God is attentive to us. There is a lot of time and space between Job and the Gospels—centuries have passed. There have been wars, kings, prophets, and exiles. The people have been refugees—vassals of empires. Maybe by the time Jesus came around God had become used to our self-centered, anthropocentric ways and just wanted to get across to us that God loves us. If we need to hear "You are more important than the sparrow," so be it—whatever it takes. It's hard getting things across to us sometimes, and mostly Jesus just wants us to know we are loved and that we don't have to be afraid.

And he hopes, knowing that, we can stop being so narcissistic and selfish—we'll be freer to love and care and be faithful like God is.

We would be rash, though, to rush over the part where Jesus says, "Not one sparrow is forgotten in the sight of God." Maybe it's hyperbole—an exaggeration to convince us of God's watchfulness, but I like it—all this profuse care. It makes God seem so warmhearted and thorough—*not one sparrow is forgotten by God.*

It also makes it seem like God must be utterly heartbroken all the time. Or maniacally stressed out or emotionally exhausted. I mean, can you imagine? I have two children—*two,* that I never forget. I have not numbered their hairs, but I understand the sentiment. Miles is DRIVING A CAR, sometimes with other teenage boys. I know that he eats fast food sometimes and that he's not getting enough broccoli and kale. Olivia just turned thirteen. Her friends don't read and sometimes they are mean. No matter how much I try to convince her she's beautiful, she can't hear it from me. Either of them could get cancer at any moment. They will be hurt by people and by unrestrained systems of power.

I don't know how God could possibly do it—manage caring so much, for so many. I don't think it is because God is especially stoic or cool. That's not the image portrayed by the Scriptures. God gets worked up about the widows and the orphans. God is passionate for God's people and the Behemoth and the wild horse. But the God who has an eye on the sparrow must be more relaxed about it all than I am capable of being—like God knows something that it is hard for us to know. Maybe that is what God is trying to get through to us—something beyond what we normally see that God would like us to glimpse. Some Holy Spirit we are warned not to blaspheme against, something permeating and thorough: don't be afraid. The sparrow thrives and falls, lives and dies, and people are often not very nice to it. *Calm* and *detached* might not be the best words to describe God, but God is not, apparently, keening uselessly in desperation, paralyzed by anxiety.

WORTHLESS SPECIES

Sparrows (and other small birds) were stripped of their feathers, threaded onto long strings, or jammed onto wooden skewers and laid out on trays all gray and lifeless to be sold in the ancient Middle Eastern marketplace as cheap food—two for a penny, according to Matthew; five for two pennies, according to Luke. (Did God's heart break?) There are dozens of sparrow species in the world, but Jesus was probably referring to the *Passer domesticus biblicus,* the Middle Eastern equivalent to the house sparrow (*Passer domesticus*), one of the most common animals in the world. They are ubiquitous. They proliferate wherever humans proliferate, and their cohabitants have not generally regarded them highly.

Field guides describe them as bland, dingy, and dull, with songs that are monotonous and grating. The Egyptian hieroglyph based on the sparrow had no phonetic value. It was used in words to indicate small, narrow, or bad. In ancient Sumerian cuneiform writing, the sparrow was the symbol for "enemy." Saint Dominic called a sparrow that interrupted his lecture the incarnation of the devil himself and then proceeded to pluck off all its feathers in front of the frightened novices while it shrieked. Worthless isn't the half of it; the bird has often inspired rage.

In the sixteenth century, a Lutheran clergyman in Germany lobbied his local government to exterminate the pesky beast. He said the sparrow's sexual promiscuity was distracting his congregation from his sermons. House sparrows do have a lot of sex. They start very young—the first chance they get, often the very first season after hatching. They aren't great parents at this age, but this doesn't keep them from copulating. House sparrows mate for life but aren't particularly chaste in their unions. Nymphomaniac witches transformed themselves into house sparrows (so some suspicious Puritan claimed) in order to fulfill their immoral drives.

The species multiplies rapidly. It is exceedingly fruitful—teeming and swarming. And though God blesses the teeming and the swarming and the multiplying in Genesis, we often find it vulgar.

House sparrows arose, evolved, and multiplied where humans arose, evolved, and multiplied. Their story is thoroughly intertwined with ours. It's often said the house sparrow is native to Europe, but it would be more accurate to say it is native to human habitat. Two jawbones found in an ancient cave in Israel suggest that the sparrow may have started cohabitating with humans as long as one hundred thousand years ago. It goes where we go. Wherever we build, it builds—or at least occupies. You can find sparrows nesting in the crevices of skyscrapers; on the bobbing heads of oil pumps; in stoplights, mines, and neon signs. They don't have a life apart from us, but we don't really like them. We treat them like drab and needy hangers-on at best, as mortal enemies at worst.

Throughout the centuries, farmers have also called for their extermination—not because of their sexual immorality, but because farmers suspected they were stealing their seeds—messing with their livelihood. In eighteenth-century England, "Sparrow Clubs" were formed with the express purpose of killing as many sparrows as possible. Some of the dead made it into sparrow pie, a popular dish across the English countryside. In Russia you could get your taxes lowered by bringing in heads of dead sparrows. Mao Tse-tung mobilized China to eradicate the tree sparrow (a similarly proliferating species) in his Four Pests Campaign. The four pests were rats, flies, sparrows, and mosquitoes. A poster for the campaign shows a boy with a slingshot poised to shoot, and a little girl with a string of dead sparrows in her hand. The caption reads "Everyone come to fight sparrows."

Chairman Mao claimed that the sparrows were robbing the people of the fruits of their labor. He rallied grandmas to bang pots and pans to keep the sparrows from landing until they dropped dead out of the sky from exhaustion. Schoolchildren tore down nests, broke eggs, and killed nestlings. Factory workers trapped and poisoned them. The People's Liberation Army shot millions of birds. Mao's campaign brought the tree sparrow to the brink of extinction in China. Some seed may have been saved, but locusts and other crop-eating insects flourished without sparrows to eat them. The resulting crop loss contributed to the Great Famine, which killed more than thirty million people.

Eventually Mao decided to take the sparrow off the list of the four pests. He included the bedbug instead.

Are not five sparrows sold for two pennies? And not one of them is forgotten by God. So fear not. You are of more value than sparrows. This seems like fairly minimal assurance, really. We can only hope we won't be poisoned or eaten.

HOUSE SPARROW DEBATES

I take a break from writing to walk the farm. I run into Diane on the driveway. She is on her way to fix the mailbox. I think she might be in a hurry, but I have been waiting for weeks to talk sparrows with her so I press ahead with my agenda. This in itself may have been mildly irritating, but I think it was also the subject. I say, "I need to talk to you about sparrows." She may not have exactly narrowed her eyes, but that's how I remember it. She asked, "What kind of sparrow?" There are all sorts of sparrows that birders are happy to discuss—the vespers, the lark, the rufous-crowned; but the house sparrow is a sore subject.

I knew that Diane and Brett had trapped and killed house sparrows in our first years on the farm. This is not an uncommon practice among birders in North America. House sparrows are aggressive. They proliferate to the detriment of native species. They compete with rarer, more beautiful birds for nesting cavities, and they usually win. When the Eastern bluebird began to disappear, bird lovers nationwide began to put up bluebird houses with the hopes of providing abundant new shelters for the endangered species. Brett and Diane put up a whole string of houses across the farm. When house sparrows began to invade these houses, the birders took measures.

I told Diane that I had read some recent reports that the house sparrow population was actually in decline. She seemed doubtful. I asked if she was starting to feel differently about the house sparrow now that the bluebirds were back. She wasn't. I wondered if she thinks the anti–house sparrow rhetoric I'd been seeing on the Internet might be a little over the top. Some of it is so scathing as to suggest that even speaking of the HOSP (an acronym for house sparrow) as if it is a real bird is like trying to pass off rotten stinking garbage for food or intimating that Hannibal Lecter is a member of the family that birders esteem. She didn't seem to think it was too terribly over the top. I let her proceed to the mailbox, feeling a little like I had come across as someone trying to defend child slavery.

The house sparrow was introduced to North America in the early 1850s. The story Jim told me, which Brett told him, was that an emigrant from England hoped to re-create his homeland in Central Park. This well-meaning but ecologically perverted soul planned to bring all the birds from Shakespeare to America to help make this rough land more livable. The house sparrow and the starling were the only ones that really took hold. "Took hold" is putting it mildly. They multiplied, teemed, and swarmed. Despite the narrative simplicity of this story, you can't actually pin the introduction of the HOSP on one lone immigrant. House sparrows were imported to various places all over the United States and Canada for various reasons: love, homesickness, to control the infestation of trees by drop worms.

Within two decades of their introduction, they had spread so far and wide that many people began to oppose their presence virulently. The Great English Sparrow Wars, a highly publicized debate among bird lovers about whether something should be done to control them, began to rage.

In their article "Dirty Birds, Filthy Immigrants, and the English Sparrow War: Metaphorical Linkage in Constructing Social Problems," Gary Alan Fine and Lazaros Christoforides (two sociologists) argue that the opponents of the house sparrow won the war hands down, in part because they linked their rhetoric to an anti-immigrant sentiment that was growing at the time.

In the decades following the Civil War, America was trying to rebuild itself and reestablish its moral ground. There was also a large influx of Asian and European immigrants at the time. When social problems arose, there was an increasing nativist tendency to blame everything on them. Foreigners were taking jobs, filling up housing, overtaking the land that rightfully belonged to Americans.

Although the Chinese had been tolerated as menial workers, when the economy declined following the war, anti-Chinese animosity grew. The idea that foreigners were endangering the good order of America became so strong that the federal government passed the Chinese Exclusion Act in 1882, one of the most significant restrictions on immigration in U.S. history. Five German immigrants were falsely blamed and summarily executed for the violence that erupted during the Haymarket Riot in Chicago in 1886. Much of the public believed it was foreigners who were radicalizing the American labor movement and inciting anarchy. Newspapers described the immigrants as arch counselors of riot, brutes, red ruffians, bloody monsters, cutthroats, thieves, assassins, and fiends. The press accused them of rioting, pillaging, and murder.

According to Fine and Christoforides, the language used against human immigrants was almost precisely duplicated in arguments against the house sparrow. Anti-sparrow activists defined the bird as "a foreigner that competes unfairly with native birds that has an immoral character and that needs to be eliminated from the American community of birds." House sparrows were "foreign vulgarians." Their homes were referred to as avian ghettos. Although the objection to the house sparrow was ostensibly economic and environmental, the folks who banded against it spent a lot of time and energy attacking the sparrow's moral character. It was accused of "filthiness, sexual immorality, dishonesty, laziness, mob violence, impudence, noisiness." Native birds were pure and wholesome. They would live peacefully in harmony if not for the foreigners among them.

The position of the anti-sparrow activists in the Great English Sparrow Wars is potently illustrated in a children's book that came out at the time titled *Citizen Bird*. The book describes a bird community where each species represents a different type of person. The house sparrow is the archetypal bad citizen. The narrative explains:

> They increased very fast and spread everywhere, quarrelling with and driving out the good citizens who belong to the regular Birdland guilds, taking their homes and

making themselves nuisances. The Wise Men protested against bringing these Sparrows, but no one heeded their warning until it was too late. Now it is decided that these Sparrows are bad Citizens and criminals; so they are condemned by every one.... This disreputable tramp not only does no work for his taxes—he hates honest work, like all vagrants—but destroys the buds of trees and plants, devours our grain crop, and drives away the industrious native birds who are good Citizens; so the Wise Men, who have tried the Sparrow's case say that he is a very bad bird, who ought to suffer the extreme penalty of the law. (Wright and Coues, 1897)

By 1887, many states had already initiated efforts to eradicate the HOSP. New York made it a misdemeanor to feed, shelter, or protect the sparrow in any way. Michigan paid a bounty of one cent per dead bird. *The Borrows Report* suggested that "all legislation protecting the sparrow be repealed; that the killing of the sparrow at all seasons of the year be made legal, including the destruction of its nests, eggs and young ... any attempt to interfere with its destruction should be made illegal."

The reputation of the house sparrow among American birders has not improved much in the last one hundred twenty years. Though their numbers by many accounts are decreasing worldwide, Americans are still waging war. I know there is no question that the reduction of biodiversity threatens the life of our planet, but I wonder if websites and blog posts that seethe with anti-HOSP rhetoric are a little misdirected—if they are directing their fear in an unhelpful direction. I have seen photos of house sparrows that look so much like police mug shots, I think the folks posting them must be skilled in propaganda arts. The HOSP looks exactly as if it had evil intent, as if it had stayed up all night doing meth. Mug shots would have this effect whether you were Brad Pitt or Amy Poehler or Julia Roberts. The boys from One Direction would look ugly and thuggish in a police photo, I'm sure of it. Some sites describe the house sparrow decapitating bluebirds to take over their nests, or its propensity to butcher babies and unborn infants.

The point, which is well taken, is to try to help people understand that if you put up birdhouses to attract native species—you may end up with only house sparrows unless you are careful—very careful, *extremely* careful, some concerned birders insist.

You can attempt deterrents first—wrapping the box in fishing line, reducing the size of the hole, or creating a "sparrow spooker" with fluttering strips of Mylar. But be warned, some of the literature persists, these "passive" methods may not only be ineffective, they may actually provoke HOSP aggression. Some people talk about HOSP revenge syndrome and HOSP rampages in response to attempts at control—rampages that leave punctured eggs and mutilated corpses in their wake. Some say there is really only one way to eliminate any possibility of a retaliatory attack—active control (i.e., kill the sparrows). I read about one woman who put them in a plastic bag and attached it to her exhaust pipe. Some traps are designed to drown them. Some people shoot them. I didn't ask Brett and Diane about their method, but the best route, according to many responsible bird lovers, is clearly active control.

All this information causes me some anxiety when the birds return in the spring. We have birdhouses in the yard that I can see from our kitchen table. It's like a parade every morning—first some goldfinches, then swallows, a rose-breasted grosbeak, mourning doves. It makes me so happy after the nearly birdless winter—until the bluebirds arrive. It appears they have occupied one of the boxes. I keep remembering a phrase from one of the websites: "Constant monitoring is essential." These are not good words for an insomniac to hear. It is better not to have boxes at all if you are not going to monitor them constantly. If you don't do everything in your power to keep the bluebirds in and the house sparrow out, then you are probably not a very good person. You have forsaken biodiversity and the life of the world.

I watch the boxes anxiously at breakfast, lunch, and dinner, every time I pass by. I lie in bed at night and ask Jim, "Do you hear a house sparrow? That sounds like a house sparrow." He says, "No, I don't think so. It's night, Debbie. The birds are sleeping." But I'm sure a HOSP will sneak in and decapitate babies when I'm not looking. I was hoping Diane might help ease my anxiety—hoping she would say she's not really worried about them anymore. I want to feel freed of the constant need for vigilance. (I don't actually know if Diane or Jim or Jesus can really help me with that, though I am still hoping.)

The next time I see Diane is at our birthday dinner. She and I have birthdays within a week of each other, so the other women on the farm always make us dinner to celebrate. I got together with Jim at Diane and Brett's wedding. We had our first babies seven days apart. Despite healthy pregnancies, both of our children ended up in the very same ICU in Minneapolis. Diane and I are both from Iowa, and we both grew up in the same small conservative denomination. When Pastor Ben left my church in Kokomo, he went to her church in Ames. I admire and respect Diane, and I love that our lives are so incredibly intertwined. I swear I am not going to cause any tension by bringing up the house sparrow again.

Linda makes us drinks with blood orange and local organic gin. Cyndy lived in China for two years. She makes the best pot stickers I have ever tasted, green beans with garlic and pork, and a crisp cucumber salad with carrots and ginger. Before Linda whips the cream for her *petits pots de crème au chocolat*—I do it again—I bring up the house sparrow. I say it's not really the sparrows' fault that they proliferate to the detriment of native species. I say it's our fault really. We destroy native bird habitat and build the sorts of places where house sparrows thrive. Maybe we shouldn't call them an invasive alien species: maybe we should call them a human-dependent species. Maybe we should blame ourselves. Maybe we're not so great. I go on and on, barely pausing to take a breath, possibly slurring my words. Finally, Diane erupts, "I know this, Debbie. I know this! You really don't have to convince me that humans are responsible! I am totally pro–birth control!" (She is, in fact, a women's health-care practitioner.) "I believe in protecting the wetlands from development!—I understand everything you are saying, but you can't kill humans! You can kill house sparrows!"

Later in the week, Jim and I give Brett a ride home from the cities. He says, a little impishly, "I saw a house sparrow in my bush the other day, and I thought, well, maybe that would make Jesus happy, but not me." He rants a little about their ugly little squished-up faces and their annoying cheeps. It's apparent to me that he and Diane have been talking, and I am afraid I have aligned myself with the enemy. I wish the bluebirds had not already moved into the house in our backyard. I don't want a sparrow war.

WORLD SPARROW DAY

Nearly everywhere the house sparrow has gone, people have wanted to kill it. It isn't just good American birders who have found it morally reprehensible. Mao, the German clergyman, English farmers, all wanted to be rid of it; but in places where it's disappearing, people are starting to love it again.

The house sparrow is rarely seen these days in London, Paris, or Mumbai. Across the United Kingdom its population has dramatically declined—by as much as 90 percent in the last thirty years. One English newspaper offered a reward to anyone who could find the reason. The paper received loads of letters in response. Some people blamed the Chernobyl disaster. Some blamed cats, sparrow hawks, magpies, or peanuts in bird feeders. A recent article in the UK's *Daily Mail* blames malaria spread by mosquitoes that are feasting beyond their usual territory due to climate change.

An environmentalist from Mumbai, Mohammed E. Dilawar, declared March 20, 2010, the first World Sparrow Day. He recruited NGOs, conservation groups, and children's magazines from India, Africa, Singapore, and Europe, hoping to raise public awareness around the globe about the decline of the house sparrow. In 2011 organizers tied the second World Sparrow Day to the ancient Hindu Holi festival, a playful celebration of spring and the marvels of color. On Holi, people go around throwing vibrant orange, red, blue, green, and beautiful pink powders at one another and rub each other's faces with scented perfume. I have only seen pictures, but I am amazed how gorgeous it all looks—everyone drenched in color, laughing, playful, mischievous. Social ties are rejuvenated at Holi. The social gap is bridged—people greet one another sweetly. It is a festival that celebrates the triumph of divine love.

Dilawar called upon people to observe Holi for house sparrows: "Sparrow Holi"—to honor the beauty of the house sparrow—the *beauty* of the house sparrow. Sparrow Holi: wow, what a beautiful crazy thing.

On the eve of World Sparrow Day 2012, the *Times* of India interviewed Gita Randhawa, a bird lover in Kanpur. She said she was thrilled, *thrilled,* to see a full flock of sparrows as she sat beside a bridge over the Ganges. Imagine that. She suggested that people should keep bowls of water on their terraces and windowsills to save sparrows from dying of thirst. Another bird lover said he longed to hear the sparrows chirp again. "Spare a thought for a sparrow," he said. "We should all do our part to bring them back—make nesting boxes with holes that are just big enough for sparrows to enter. Put out the right sort of seed to attract them."

I love this. It seems beautiful to me—but what irony. We despise what is common and love what is rare. Is this inevitable?

Is this just the way it goes—hate, hate, hate, love, hate, love, hate, hate love? Is it just true that love comes in fits and starts and almost always erratically?

BREEDING COMPASSION

Praying mantises eat their lovers while they mate. Mother lions occasionally devour the dead carcasses of their babies. I have heard of beloved dogs that maul the faces of their masters. House sparrows kill bluebirds. Still, I don't think Jesus would take back his words: not one sparrow is forgotten by God. Maybe it's meant to be a threat: they will all be punished—thrown into unquenchable fire for their sin. But somehow I doubt that is the gist of it.

God cares for what the world considers insignificant. This is all over the text: the weak and the poor, the widows, the broken. Jesus eats with the common people. God's eye is on the sparrow. Our eyes are so often on something with a little more prestige. Our culture worships stars. People strive for fame as if it is truly a worthwhile pursuit. We desperately don't want to be *common*, as if we still cling to class divisions established in antiquity. We don't like what is common—we are so much more attracted to what is shiny and rare. We are hardly able to convince ourselves that God is unlike us in this.

But the Scripture keeps pressing us to hear this: God loves what is ubiquitous. God loves the world—every single part of it—the bland, the ugly, the dingy squishy-faced, the monotonous and grating. There is no way in which God reserves God's love for what the world finds beautiful or important. God loves the sinner. I believe God might like for us to have some of this love. Have it and share it—widely, all around.

It would be good for the world if we could, somehow, delight in the everyday, the everyman, what presses up against us incessantly—our spouses and neighbors. This seems to be right up there on God's list (as if God really has a list): the Great Commandment is "Love God; love your neighbor"; love what is ever present. Maybe people wanted a mighty, fancy, elite sort of God. God gave them Jesus, who consorted with the commoners, died with thieves. And still we've (sometimes) tried to make him out to be a superhuman—but I wonder if the point somehow is more about the ordinary. It's not the love of the sacred that will save the world as much as the embracing of the profane.

Apuleius, the ancient poet and philosopher, said a thousand years ago that familiarity breeds contempt. I think we might suffer from this—in our communities, and in our most intimate relationships. Apparently some companies try to guard against familiarity breeding contempt. They maintain that management should keep its distance from employees in order to retain respect. Maybe this works for corporations whose main goal is profit, but it doesn't seem like a great strategy to help us get along in the world generally. We need one another too much. Ostriches can walk and feed themselves the day they hatch—we need parents to help us for years. We are extremely interdependent beings.

The idea that familiarity breeds contempt isn't lost on me; I just think it might be nice to learn a different way of being. It isn't difficult to find hateable qualities in the creatures that surround us. And I don't think it's just egregious misbehaviors that rankle us. It is not only that the house sparrow is aggressive, or that its chirps are objectively horrible; it's more that they are just so ever present.

I have noticed a lot of people posting on Facebook for their wedding anniversaries. People say things like "Twenty-three years, and I still feel the same way about my wife as I did on the day we met." This is vaguely disturbing to me. I find it hard to believe. The intertwining of daily lives (cleaning, money, chewing, loading the dishwasher) seems much more complicated than that to me. Intimacy changes love. A lot.

When I first met my husband, he was caring for his grandmother. He had a little studio on her farm where he painted. He made her dinner, got the mail, cleaned the kitchen, watched birds. He had no other job and no money. When we went out for breakfast after Brett and Diane's wedding, the morning after we had first kissed, he asked me if I could pay because he didn't have any money. I found this utterly and completely—devastatingly—charming, this beautiful artist man who lived outside the system that runs the world. When he left his MFA program in Brooklyn, he threw all his paintings into a Dumpster. I was in love with his freedom to disregard societal convention.

I still love and respect his countercultural tendencies, but I have come to discover that it's not all about some stunning freedom. Sometimes I wish he would have kept a few of those paintings or at least tried to sell them to a gallery. And quite frankly, I don't like the noisy way he repeatedly stabs his plate with his fork when he is just trying to capture a little broccoli.

When you live right up next to something day after day for a very long time, it looks different than the first time you saw it. Love God. Love your neighbor as yourself—this is a whole different prospect than loving what is rare.

Twenty years ago I thought my husband was singularly blessed, like my friends, all golden and shimmery; and we were poised to create the most beautiful community together. I don't think any of us feel quite like we did when we began. But I do think there is something about what we have done together that allows us to sustain one another, as well as our children and the land we've settled on.

It's not difficult to hate things, really. It's so easy to enumerate the unlikable qualities of other residents on our planet: our next-door neighbors, our spouses, the Republicans, the Democrats, Michelle Bachmann, Barack Obama. I actually think people spend a lot of time doing this. I certainly have. People have habits that are hard for other people to respect. But I don't think generating hate ever results in more good, or more love, or more compassion. This seems so obvious, but we keep doing it again and again, thinking that it will somehow be for the good if we can finely hone our critiques—perfect a scathing rant.

We are all potentially hateable. I think this is one of our biggest fears—that we are actually worthless. We are not good. We are irritating. We have nothing new to say. We are tiresome and mundane. There is no one I find as tiresome as myself. Talk about ubiquitous. It's so difficult to find someplace quiet apart from myself, hard to keep me out of the room for even a moment. I just keep following myself around wherever I go, monotonously chirping.

But what we need so desperately to feel is love—if not passion, then at least some more abundant compassion. We need to cultivate patience, love, and understanding for the good of our marriages and neighborhoods and nature and the universe—duh. But somehow we go on and on, acting as if this is not obvious at all—we harbor disgust; we delight in scapegoating; we are so angry about everyone's moral degeneracy. Or we find it hilarious and bond with our friends against the loathsome, or the ridiculous, or people who are weirdly dressed.

Maybe hatred is so easy because we don't feel that good about ourselves. We are afraid somewhere that we might be worthless, common—as if common is a terrible thing to be, but we hide this fear at every turn. Otherwise, people might catch on, begin to see it themselves—our worthlessness. Maybe it's the hiding of our own self-hatred that makes us hate others. There are psychoanalysts and philosophers who would back me up on this.

But I am completely taken with Jesus' stance toward the unlovable and the seemingly worthless. I really believe this is the kind of God we need. A God that is attentive to the sparrow.

In Psalm 84, the psalmist sings of God's sanctuary, about how lovely it is and about how his soul longs, yea, faints for it. His heart sings for joy to the living God who provides it—even the sparrow finds a home and the swallow a nest in this safe and beautiful place. We need the kind of God who shelters the sparrow. What other kind of God could find a place for us? There is nothing that is worthless to God, nothing that God doesn't take up in God's embrace.

In Luke, Jesus says, not one sparrow is forgotten by God.

This seems so ludicrously compassionate; but then four verses later Jesus says, "Every one who speaks a word against the Son of man will be forgiven; but he who blasphemes against the Holy Spirit will not be forgiven," and it seems like this takes a quick turn toward unmerciful. But what does it mean? What is the Holy Spirit—the spirit of forgiveness and compassion? Maybe it really isn't a threat—a warning about a line that can't be crossed. Maybe it's more of a statement about what happens—almost more like science than morality. It's about what the lack of love breeds. You may not speak well of Jesus; you may not even know of him; you may be a Hindu or a Cherokee; you may believe in Unelanuhi or Ganesh—you may still breed forgiveness, but if you blaspheme against forgiveness, you will breed something else. As humans we have a responsibility to behave in ways that breed compassion.

Can you love songbirds and still be compassionate to the house sparrow? Can you have an incisive critique without a hardening of the heart? Maybe it's tricky, not completely easy, a little complex, but we of all species are especially equipped to handle a little complexity.

LOVE THE SPARROW

The house sparrow is not necessarily dull and uninteresting. In Australia they've learned to open automatic doors. Some hover in front of the electric eye until the door opens. Others, mostly females, sit atop the electric eye and lean over until they trip the sensor.

Although not a waterbird, the house sparrow can swim if it

needs to—to escape a predator, for instance. Sparrows caught in a trap over a water dish tried to escape by diving into the water and swimming underwater from one part of the trap to another.

Our hearts beat seventy times a minute; the house sparrow's beats eight hundred. At rest we breathe about eighteen times a minute; a sparrow, ninety times. I like thinking of them breathing so fast—all this breathing out in the world, all this heartbeating.

Love your neighbor. It's the most brilliant instruction. It's wise and wonderful and something we need.

8

T H E

COCK

C O C K I N E S S *and*
B E T R A Y A L

 THE COCK IS OFTEN
referred to as "Peter's bird." If you are a
teenage boy (or, I guess, if you are me), you
might not be able to help noticing that three
of the words in the last sentence are slang for
a male body part. Peter is the rock upon
which the church is built. Once you've noticed the slang connec-
tions—this seems a little bit funny (or perhaps, not so funny
depending on where you go with it). Jesus calls Simon "Petra": the
rock, the pillar. He also calls him Satan. The rock thinks he can
walk on water, but as soon as he steps out of the boat, he sinks.

I have always imagined the cock crowing on the night of
Jesus' betrayal as a sort of feathered alarm clock, nothing more
significant. But a rooster is really nothing like a timepiece. (If
you've ever been around roosters, you know they don't crow at
anything like dependable intervals.) The rooster is the creature
that announces Peter's heartbreaking betrayal. Perhaps we lose
the impact of this if we don't consider the bird.

PETER'S BIRD

The rooster's association with the male phallus is not just a coincidence of modern slang. The link is ancient. It's hard to find a time or a culture where the cock was not associated with masculine virility. The rooster crowed at sunrise and its red crown looked like the sun's rays—the sun represented fertility, the ability to generate life. Whereas the dove often represented female sexuality, the rooster became associated with the power of the male. And it was believed that the rooster had very profound power indeed. The cock was believed to be so potent that if a man smeared himself with a broth made of boiled cock and garlic, the fiercest of beasts could not harm him. The cock was so formidable a beast that rabid lions, tigers, or bears couldn't stand before, or even look at, a cock. Even the most terrible basilisk monster would be so struck with fear at the sound of a cockcrow that it would simply die of fear. The cockcrow wasn't a PA system announcing to farmers that it was time to wake up. It epitomized the power of masculine virility.

I went to hear Sherman Alexie, one of my favorite authors, speak recently. He was profound and hilarious, but I couldn't believe how much he talked about penises and how everyone roared at these jokes. He told a woman in the audience that men think about their peters all the time, no matter the conversation, topic, or event. Afterward I asked Jim if there was truth in this. He said, "Mmm, maybe a shred." Will the phallic cult never cease?

The rooster's emphatic cock-a-doodle-doo comes at the precise place in the Gospel story where Jesus is giving up power—a move that Peter, throughout the narrative, has vehemently resisted. Jesus insists on an entirely different road to redemption, an entirely different calculus of strength and power than the one his beloved disciples continually lurch toward.

THE COCKFIGHT

One thing impossible to ignore about the rooster is that it is a fighter. The domestic chicken/rooster is descended from the wild red jungle fowl of Asia. Somewhere around six thousand years ago, maybe longer, people discovered that if you took the female red jungle fowl's eggs away, she would lay another and another and she would do this indefinitely. The males, obviously, couldn't lay eggs, but it was noted early on that they were very aggressive toward each other. Two cocks placed in close proximity, perfect strangers, will usually fight automatically and without provocation, often to the death. They even have a special weapon for this purpose—a spur on the lower leg. People started keeping hens for eggs and cocks for fighting. The bird could provide both food and entertainment. It didn't take long for the domesticated red jungle fowl to spread all over the world.

The female red jungle fowls were bred through the ages to be better and better egg layers; the broilers to be better meat; and the roosters to be better fighters. Cockfighting is said to be the oldest sport in the world. Of course there is still the run-of-the-mill barnyard rooster, but there are cocks whose bloodlines have been blended and refined with the same sort of attention the vintner gives to grapes. Mexican cocks are known for one thing; Puerto Ricans another. Avenger Farms in the Philippines offers fifteen different bloodlines, including Lemon 84, Dink Sweater, O and O, Jumper Radioline, and Owlsnest. Each bloodline manifests a particular fighting style. Some are slow, strong, and deliberate. Some go for the fast kill. Some fly high—others weave from side to side. They are all magnificent-looking birds—colorful and majestic.

I haven't thought much about cockfighting in my life up until now. If I considered it at all, I suppose I believed in some vague way that its practitioners must be the same sort of people who would skin puppies for pleasure. I didn't think there were many of them. I assumed it was some perversion that existed among miscreants and gangsters in some dark and seedy crack of civilization. I presumed wrong.

The fighting cock was an object of worship among the Babylonians. "Spiritual" cockfights took place outside temples in India. The Greeks used cockfights for gambling, religious ceremonies, and training soldiers for battle. Socrates' last words, according to Plato, were "I owe a cock to Asclepios, Crito. Pay him without fail." We're talking Socrates—not exactly a villainous malfeasant. One of the oldest representations of a fighting cock was found during the excavation of Mizpah, a biblical city near Jerusalem. It dates from the sixth century BCE. The bones of fighting roosters have been found all over the ruins of the ancient Holy Land. The Romans took to the sport like ducks to water. The fighting cock, like the empire, championed machismo, took its enemies down through brute force, and displayed a vigorous ferocity.

Although cockfighting is now illegal in every state in our

nation, this is a fairly recent development, and it is still practiced down dirt roads in California and in basements in New York City. In countries where it is legal—the Philippines, Bali, Puerto Rico, Mexico, and Peru, for example—it is a major national pastime. Wherever, whenever, however cockfighting is practiced, it is almost always an exclusively male activity. Across cultures, when a rooster backs away from the ring or refuses to fight, it is called a runaway chicken. If a cock is badly hurt in the ring and begins to make clucking noises, it is said to be "crying like a chicken." In the midst of the fight, if a bird is not doing well, onlookers often comment that "the mother's blood is showing." A good cock does not show any weakness. It does not display any henlike qualities. Winning cocks, say the breeders, display markers of a "real" man. They are assertive, courageous, tenacious, fierce, belligerent, virile, dominant, and strong.

In a famous essay on cockfighting in Bali, "Deep Play: Notes on the Balinese Cockfight," Clifford Geertz, an anthropologist, discusses how important cockfights are to social structure:

As much of America surfaces in a ballpark, on a golf links, at a racetrack, or around a poker table, much of Bali surfaces in a cock ring. For it is only apparently cocks that are fighting there. Actually, it is men. To anyone who has been in Bali any length of time, the deep psychological identification of Balinese men with their cocks is unmistakable. The double entendre here is deliberate.... The fact that they are masculine symbols par excellence is about as indubitable, and to the Balinese about as evident, as the fact that water runs downhill.

Geertz observed that the cockfight brings together themes of animal savagery, male narcissism, status rivalry, and blood sacrifice.

Sometimes a cockfight is over in a matter of minutes, sometimes it takes awhile. The weaker bird loses, most often dies—the stronger one prevails, again and again. The winning cock stands on top of its dead opponent in the middle of the pit and crows its victory into the air. Maybe this is the bird Peter hears. The bird that is emblematic of his betrayal. The signal that he has not yet shaken his devotion to the empire's calculus.

The connection of the rooster to certain definitions of manliness is ancient and prevalent—a version that is tied to violence, one that champions competition. Jesus may not be the chicken who runs, but he's not going to fight. Earlier, Peter voiced his objection to the notion that Christ's mission might go in this direction. Jesus called him Satan. Peter couldn't be faithful to the direction things were going. The cock crows, and suddenly his betrayal becomes clear.

REAL MEN

Some church leaders, concerned that the church does not attract males, have pressed lately for a reading of Scripture that emphasizes that Jesus was a "real man." If the church is to survive, the proponents of the masculinity movement claim, its leaders must reclaim their manhood. I probably shouldn't have started perusing their websites or watching their videos. Jesus wasn't a gentle man, they say—he was more of a champion cock: aggressive, competitive, brave, cocky—like the Mexicans say of their best roosters, "tiene cojones."

Although Jesus certainly seems to part ways with religious authorities and the Roman rule, and though he certainly seems to walk through the world without much fear, I can't read him like a cock. His fearlessness seems to have more to do with trust than some sort of cockiness. It has to do with being able to be in the place of shame with no shame, as James Alison says. The Romans were the guys that believed in machismo. It is a culture that Jesus challenges rather than endorses. Jesus teaches his disciples that they need to die to self. That seems like a wildly and beautifully different approach to manhood than the one found in the cockfighting culture.

WHO'S THE GREATEST

I'm often disappointed that the disciples aren't more developed as characters in the Gospels. We have no idea what they look like or how old they are. We know that some of them were fishermen, but mostly they are nondescript. They are men who followed Jesus around as a group. Their personalities are secondary.

I've often imagined them as grown men, but maybe they were more like postpubescent teenagers, walking around with their hoods up and their jeans down low. Any seminormal Jewish man was married by eighteen, had kids. Other than Peter's mother-in-law, there's no mention in the Gospels of wives or children. The disciples leave their jobs to start following this guy around who crosses boundaries, breaks rules—a man the authorities find suspicious, even dangerous. Maybe they were a little like a roving band of young punks. Their mothers were probably worried about them. But maybe the boys feel some budding sense of exhilarating freedom, out from under the gaze of their parents, running with an outlaw. Pretty soon they're galloping through the fields plucking grain on the Sabbath. They're smoking cigarettes on the temple steps. They're sitting down to eat a meal in front of the most careful couriers of the sacred Law, and *they aren't washing their hands before they eat*. It certainly seems impolite, vaguely immature.

Jesus tells them that "whatever goes into a man from outside can't defile him." That seems like a reckless thing to tell a group of teenage boys. There are a lot of things from the outside they might like to try to put in. They don't seem to have a very firm grasp of what's going on around them. They follow Jesus, but they never seem to understand where he's leading. Maybe that's a little what it's like to be a disciple. You spend a lot of time confused. You have a lot to learn.

One of the funniest (or saddest, depending on how you look at it) things the disciples do is argue repeatedly over who is the greatest. It's like they can't help breaking out into these little cockfights—often at the most inopportune times. There may be some tragedy in this, but it kind of cracks me up because there is some Three Stooges sort of surreal honking-and-butting absurdity in it as well.

When they are passing through Galilee, Jesus begins to teach them, Mark says, that he is going to be delivered into the hands of men (rather than, say, heroically defeat his enemies). Men are going to kill him and he's going to let them. He isn't going to fight back. After Jesus explains this, the disciples immediately break out into a little cockfight. The juxtaposition is meaning-full. The boys don't respond to Jesus' message; instead they start vying for a place of power, arguing over who is the greatest.

Mark says that they didn't understand and they were afraid to ask. They were afraid. I can understand this—it seems scary, but the disciples don't articulate their fears or their lack of understanding. They don't show compassion or put their arms around Jesus and say, "Oh, no." Instead, they start comparing sizes.

Jesus doesn't really reprimand them, but he puts things in a different perspective. He says, "Whoever wants to be first must be least of all and the servant of all." This is not really a new bit of information for them, but it is something he seems to need to constantly repeat. Then he takes a child and puts the child in the midst of them and takes the child in his arms and says, "Whoever receives one such child receives me; and whoever receives me, receives not me but the one who sent me." If I've mentioned this before, it's because I can't quite get over it. It says something very significant about the one who sent him, something rather shocking about who he is, who God is, and how God works in the world. The God that Jesus reveals doesn't seem bent on manifesting power as we conceive of power. The disciples of Jesus only rarely seem to grasp this, if at all.

Again, I don't know if it's funny or tragic or a little of both, but it happens again in the middle of the Last Supper; a cockfight breaks out in the room on the second floor. Jesus breaks the bread and says, "This is my body, which is given for you." He pours the wine and says, "This cup is the new covenant by my blood, which is poured out for you." And then, "For the Son of man goes as it has been determined; but woe to that man by whom he is betrayed!"

The disciples start to question one another, which of them would do this, and lo and behold, says Luke, "a dispute also arose among them, which of them was to be regarded as the greatest."

I wonder what these arguments over who was the greatest looked like. Who was the biggest, or who was smartest, or who had the best ideas, who was the most well-liked? It seems like lunacy, and I think we all do it—maybe not outright, but as a sort of running commentary in our heads. We waste a lot of time worrying about where we fit in some phantom hierarchy. I am not a teenage boy. I am a grown woman, but I do it a lot. It's exhausting.

"Woe to the man by whom he is betrayed." I believe this includes all of us. We resist the direction Jesus leads. We want to be the greatest and hang out with the greatest. We don't want to be counted among the least. We want to win all our fights in the ring.

WHERE COMPETITION LEADS

We live in a culture that believes in competition, trusts it somehow to make things better. Companies will be spurred by competition to make the best possible product. Athletes will run faster; people will *try* harder. The best will win. Maybe competition works well in games—high school football players get pumped imagining their rivals—but I'm not sure it's worked out that well for the life of the world. The majority of companies are not striving to make the best product—they are trying to make something as cheaply as possible that will sell. They are trying to make money.

Our candidates for public office are obliged to speak of the nation's need to compete. I don't think they mean we need to be the most generous nation; they mean we need to be as powerful as possible and make as much money as we can. If our nation competing means passing austerity measures that will leave the poor without food, shelter, or health care, so be it. It may mean we have to dredge up oil, cut down trees, and pollute rivers with industrial waste. The need to win may keep us from putting a cap on our carbon emissions. This may work out well for Big Oil, but the planet is gasping for breath: competition has exhausted and depleted it.

In a recent article in *Harper's,* David Samuels suggests that though the yearning for nature, for wilderness, still exists in humans, we will need to adjust, because there is no wild left, really. We have ushered in a new epoch—the Anthropocene: the age of man. We've had our hands all over everything. The forest, the bears, the tigers are nearly all gone. The wild has lost. Other species are dying out by the minute. We have outrun everything. But you cannot call this winning. An eminent biologist who helped to eradicate smallpox from this planet said recently that he believes humans will become extinct within the next hundred years. He may be wrong, but he's clearly not a lunatic.

Our unflagging belief in competition is often rooted in the idea that it is an evolutionary necessity, but Darwin adopted the phrase "survival of the fittest" at the height of the Industrial Revolution. It was a brutal, ruthless, competitive age—and although, even then, Darwin really meant "fit" in the sense of "appropriate" (what fits best in a space), we've come to think of it more as "survival of the strongest," the most muscular. We have used his theories to justify the callous nature of economics and the notion that might is right.

We've used Darwin to justify the idea that human beings are locked into competition for our survival, but that take on things is a bit outdated. Nature can be competitive, but there is a whole different side to the story. Nature is also incredibly cooperative. Atoms cooperate by combining to make up molecules. The components in a cell work together to keep it living. We live in a complex, interdependent universe:

> The more that scientists look at the way the world operates—at the science of ecology—the more they perceive the key principle of interdependence, not only between creature and creature, but also between life as a whole and the fabric of the planet. Our individual bodies—trillions of cells working in harmony, each answering to the calls of 30,000 genes…are a master class in cooperation. More and more, too, biologists are finding cooperativeness within populations of animals and between animals of different species that share the same habitat. If the universe were not more cooperative than it is competitive, it would fall apart.

I don't think this would be news to Jesus or Buddha, Gandhi or the Dalai Lama, but it seems to be news most humans still need to hear. We need to let it sink in before it's too late. When the cock crows in the Gospels, it isn't a sign of victory—it is the sound that underlines human betrayal.

HEARTBREAKING STORIES

The Scripture is full of heartbreaking stories. The world is made and it's beautiful and lovely and everyone's naked in the garden together in love, but then there's deception and fear and separation and not-love, and Adam and Eve start hiding and lying and then one of their children ends up killing the other. And there's Joseph's very own brothers throwing him into a pit in the wilderness and leaving him there. And there's Judas falling in love with Jesus, getting disappointed in him, then betraying him, and then in devastating regret, hanging himself. Heartbreaking. There's the woman who wets Jesus' feet with her tears and wipes them with her hair. If you went through the Bible and tried to sort it according to categories, like "Teachings on How to Behave Well," or "How to Start a Revolution," maybe "Pious Ranting," the "Heartbreaking Story" category would far exceed the others.

Why are there so many heartbreaking stories? Maybe because there is no redemption without brokenness. Your heart can't be recreated out of mercy and love if it is thoroughly intact. Peter's story is heartbreaking. He stands out among the disciples. He is definitely a character you can get a feel for, though people's feelings about him may differ. You can read him as someone who has a lot of sweet enthusiasm—a lot of energy and passion, almost like a puppy dog. He is a little impetuous, but naively so—never maliciously. He's always right there with Jesus, enthusiastically following, ready to throw himself over the side of the boat, ready to defend Jesus against any notion of failure. You could say that he is loyal, brave, fierce in his faith; and you could find this all very endearing.

On the other hand, you could read him as a little cocky. The cock is Peter's bird. He thinks he can walk on water? Really? When Jesus is transfigured on the mountain, Peter's reaction is to want to build something. When Jesus says he's going to die, Peter says, "Never!" He may think he's being faithful, but it's apparent from the story that Peter has a skewed impression about what that means.

At the Last Supper, when the other disciples are fighting, Peter promises Jesus—he insists: "Even though they all fall away, I will not." In other words, "Everyone else may leave you, but I never will." You could read him as earnest and well-intentioned. You could also read him as a bit of a show-off, a piece of work—all braggadocio. Maybe he's not all puppy dog—maybe he's just a little bit Tony Soprano.

Peter vows he is loyal. Jesus says, "Truly, I say to you, this very night, before the cock crows twice, you will deny me three times." Peter comes back vehemently, "If I must die with you, I will not deny you." He overestimates himself. Or maybe he lies. Maybe there's not that much difference between the two. He says he will never ever deny Jesus no matter what, and in the next moment he's doing it again and again. He abandons Jesus in Jesus' most painful and needful moment.

Of all the betrayals at Jesus' death, Peter's is the most heart-breaking. The religious authorities think they are protecting their religion. The empire behaves the way you expect the empire to behave. The big powerful forces share responsibility for killing the unconditional Lover of the world, but there's something about the part they play that seems intelligible. Even if the government or the moral authorities condemn you, you really need your friends to love you.

Peter's offense may be the least in terms of the actual legal proceedings that lead to the death of Jesus, but it's the most painful. Peter betrays the one he professes to love. The last we hear of Peter in the book of Mark is that after having denied Jesus three times, he "remembered how Jesus had said to him, 'Before the cock crows twice, you will deny me three times.' And [Peter] broke down and wept." And that's it, the last of Peter in Mark's Gospel. This is the legacy of the Christian church; the rock upon which it is built is broken. This seems like a fairly crucial revelation.

LOSING OUR SELVES

There's something shattering about the gospel. Maybe because our understating, our educations, our imaginations, the structures of our consciousnesses, our selves have been formed so thoroughly by forces other than love and mutuality and mercy and empathy and tolerance, that they need to be lost or shattered—our selves as they have been formed by the kingdoms of the world. Jesus says, "I will lead you somewhere else, and this place is going to involve losing your self, not your soul, but your self—the self that is bent on rivalry and competition, the self that needs to believe you are better than other people, the self that builds itself up at the expense of others."

When Jesus says, "Deny yourself, follow me"—he's calling into being a different sort of self, a self that is formed by the love of God, mercy, mutuality, and empathy. Jesus is calling us all to come to be something that stretches us out of our old selves, beyond our limits. He wants to give us eyes to see, ears to hear. He wants us to wake up and open up. This may hurt because we won't be able to separate ourselves from or exclude the suffering and the poor and the sick and the broken, and that won't feel exactly painless. It will open our hearts to love and unbelievable mercy, which means unbelievable empathy—which means a heart broken open.

What is strong and powerful, rich and hard, doesn't break open so easily. Not that it's impossible, but it is easier for a camel to go through the eye of a needle than for a rich man to enter the kingdom of God. That is how it is. It is what is vulnerable that can allow itself to be broken, or is broken, so that it can be re-created, be made again.

FREEDOM

I don't think the story of the disciples' betrayal is meant to get us thinking, *Ohhh man, if only the disciples had been better people—if only they'd stuck by Jesus, if only they'd behaved better, or believed better. If only they weren't so self-centered, power-seeking, uncomprehending, and lost*. The revelation of the abandonment and the betrayal is an essential part of the story for us to hear.

It's fitting that the Last Supper, the meal we reenact in the church every week, includes the disciples' fighting and betrayal. His followers must have had some sense that it was important to include this in their stories, because they do. They are the ones who pass down these narratives where, in the climactic moment, they don't look very good. They look foolish fighting, like roosters in the ring. They abandon Jesus. They don't look faithful. They look like people who need mercy. And maybe they were okay with looking like that because they came to know that mercy is what the world needs. Maybe that's mostly what disciples are: people who need mercy.

The disciples don't look like winners in the stories they tell to spread the gospel. They have mostly small parts in the drama, and none of them are heroes. Somewhere along the line they must have gotten free from that thing that made them need to fight to be the greatest. Maybe there is something about discipleship that ends up looking like that: the freedom to tell a story where you don't look good. Maybe there's something essential about that. Perhaps it's this freedom that helps to spread the good news. It's the opposite of cockiness.

The church is not being a very good witness if it doesn't take to heart its betrayal and confess it—maybe even constantly. The cock is Peter's bird. It's the bird of betrayal. Peter is the rock upon which church is built—it's not a very impressive rock, really. I think this is beautiful. The rock is broken.

At the end of the Gospel stories, Peter is not strutting like a cock. He weeps. Maybe he is not quite "crying like a chicken," but we do glimpse a different side of Peter than the one he has tried to project. He is not made as fierce as possible as a disciple of Jesus. He is not trained to put on a good show in the ring. Jesus is not this kind of trainer. He does not impress us with his ability to do violence to others. He lays down his life, his sword—he walks out of the ring, so that we may likewise be free to do so. Imagine the space that might open up outside the sphere of competition, what might grow outside the confines of the ring.

9

T H E

HEN

F R E E D O M *and*
D O M E S T I C A T I O N

IT'S A BIT SHOCKING that of all the birds Jesus might have identified himself with, he picked the chicken. He might have chosen something glorious—the splendid fairy wren, the lammergeier, a sunbird, a spider catcher might have been a nice metaphor, a bird with a beautiful song or huge strong wings. But out of all the dazzling colorful possibilities—he compares himself to a hen.

"O Jerusalem, Jerusalem, killing the prophets and stoning those who are sent to you! How often would I have gathered your children together as a hen gathers her brood under her wings, and you would not!"

It's a loving image, but it's not especially dignified. The chicken is not a magnificent bird—it is the most domesticated animal there is. A hen is a fussy old woman—a fat-bottomed grandma in an apron pickling cucumbers. Chicken is what you find sitting on Styrofoam, wrapped in plastic in the meat department at the grocery store. I remember the pale boy with dark brown hair my son invited to his eighth birthday party. He lived in the trailer park and he didn't have a father and he wouldn't climb the ladder to the loft where the other boys were playing. They taunted him until he was in tears, "Chicken, bak bak, chicken, bak, bak, chicken . . ." I intervened, but I'm afraid it only made matters worse—as if a young man shouldn't need protecting. It is vastly different to be a chicken than it is to be a cock, in the schoolyard, at a party in junior high. I have done plenty of things to avoid the title myself.

COMMUNITY CHICKENS

We decided as a community to raise chickens. For some of us the stimulus was paranoia about potential apocalypse (peak oil, climate change, class warfare). For others it was about creating a good experience for the children. We all grow vegetables, freeze and can. We liked the idea of raising a protein source on our own as well.

I liked the idea of having chickens—the kids going to the roost to collect fresh eggs for breakfast, a step toward self-sufficiency, but in truth I find them appalling—the way their crap piles up in the roost, the way they lay eggs on their own piles of poop, the way they eat their own eggs or peck one another to death. When I put the chickens in one night, mice scattered across my feet from the feedbag. Gathering eggs was all right, but cleaning the coop seemed insurmountable. I was sure someone in my family would end up with salmonella or bird flu.

A weasel slaughtered the first round of our chickens. It got into the coop somehow and killed them all. It left the carcasses. The second round ranged freely for a time, until the dogs picked them off one by one. There was one poor hen that was beaten and pecked so fiercely by the others that Dana made her a special shelter by his house. She just stayed inside and quietly died. It's very disturbing to look at a chicken that has been pecked. I hated how it made my daughter Olivia's heart ache—the strong ones beating up the weak one. I hated how it reinforced the notion of survival of the fittest before my children's eyes. The meek and the weak will perish at the beaks of the strong. The kids named her Rosie.

My family opted out of the third round of chickens. I have mixed feelings about it. Jim keeps talking about building our own coop behind his studio. Like so many things in community, it seems that it would be easier to do it on our own, though this is sort of the reverse of what community is supposed to be. We won't have to worry about whose turn it is to clean the coop or feel wrenching guilt that we haven't done our part. When the community dogs die (all six of them), we could let them range free.

Chicken salad, chicken cordon bleu, Kentucky-fried. We boil chicken feet to make chicken stock. Jennette, our friend who is a natural foods educator, says it is one of the most nutritious things you can do, but they look eerie bouncing up and down in the pot on the stove.

Pliny writes of those who first devised to "cram" hens to fatness, from which "arose that detestable gourmandise and gluttonie to eat Hens and Capons so fat and enterlarded with their owne grease." He regrets that we began to "keepe foules within narrow coups and cages as prisoners, to which creatures Nature had allowed the wide aire for their scope and habitation." But he goes on to give rules for raising chickens and preserving eggs. He claims that a man named Galerius owned a chicken that could talk. He says that in Egypt eggs were hatched in manure beds. Chickens today are eons away from the wild red jungle fowls from which they came. We have not only changed the chicken's lifestyle, penned it in, we have reconstructed it as a species. Perhaps Jesus was prescient when he compared himself to a hen; we have certainly had our way with him—caging and packaging.

THE COOP

Spring started in March this year. It is three months later and we still don't have mosquitoes. This is unprecedented in the twenty years I've lived in Minnesota. Usually there are two hours or so between when the snow is gone and the mosquitoes come. I'm sure it has something to do with catastrophic climate change, but I've decided that we might as well enjoy the few moments of existence we have left. It's hard to maintain pessimism because of the birds. They have come back in multitudes. We have eighty-three acres of mixed fields, woods, and riverside. I know this must be wildly inaccurate, but it feels like there are ten birds per square yard. The world is bursting with birds. Their sounds change the atmosphere. They buzz and tweet and squawk and chirp and honk and grunt and sing and coo and whistle and rattle and twill and I can hardly believe we don't die of it—all the beauty. I can't believe we aren't all going around fainting in awe or grabbing our friends or calling people up all over: "Have you heard?"

I have been walking our trails, sometimes even twice a day, to try to absorb it. I don't care if the birds are common, invasive, or rare. I am dazzled by the life. I am grateful every time I get a good look through the binoculars, but even if I can't quite focus—I don't care. There are colorful jewels flying around and singing. It's outrageous. When I think I'm as smitten as possible, three huge sandhill cranes fly low over my head. It seems like God is orchestrating this spectacle—maybe showing off a little: look what I made, isn't it the most amazing creation ever?

The path around the north pasture takes me by the chicken coop. It's almost like passing a concentration camp in comparison. One day Brett is out fixing the mower when Jim and I walk by. He asks us if we want to see his new broilers. He is proud of them. They aren't cute and fuzzy anymore like they were when he first got them, but he likes them. They are molting and they have bare pink skin in places. They are ugly to me. I try to like them, but mostly I just feel sorry for them because set beside the birds of spring they look pathetic. The broilers are bred to be obese, says Brett. Pretty soon they will all get so fat they will barely be able to walk. It's not a matter of them overeating. Even if they got more exercise, they would still get fat. It's in their genes. I ask Brett, "So, really? They gain weight no matter what they do or what they eat?" I say, "That's terribly unfair. They must resent it *very* deeply."

The layers are much better looking than the broilers, but equally sad to me. They lay eggs that will never hatch. If a layer begins to sit on her nest to incubate her eggs (what would come natural to any mother), she is said to have gone "broody." A broody hen can disrupt the laying cycle of the whole coop and thus must be broken of the habit immediately.

Chicken *meat* is even a little sad, if you ask me. My colleague always says you should never order the chicken in a nice restaurant. Only rarely does the chef recommend it. It is called a "neutral foodstuff." That just doesn't sound good. Nearly half of the chicken found in U.S. grocery stores is contaminated with *Staphylococcus aureus* bacteria. That doesn't sound good either. I know a lot of people are crazy about hot chicken wings. This has never made any sense to me.

BEULAH

The Chicken Lady began as a repeating and unrelenting image in Sonja's dreams—an old woman washing and butchering chickens. The dreams kept coming so Sonja, an artist in my congregation, decided to pay attention to them, incorporating the Chicken Lady into her art. She named the woman Beulah and gave her a story. She has created sculptures and artifacts related to Beulah's life.

Beulah, in Sonja's building narrative of her, is an old Norwegian farm wife who had a sacred revelation while dissecting a chicken. Sonja says, "The curtain was pulled back and Beulah saw God." Sonja can't describe the precise nature of the revelation, but she expressed it in these words: *God is in the kitchen; God is in the chicken.*

Sonja's mother died of cancer when Sonja was twenty-three. She began to deal with the layers of her grief in her art, using the metaphor of birds. At home, in the fall when the birds began to migrate, Sonja and her mother would stop whatever they were doing and go out to watch the "never-ending black ribbon of birds flying overhead." Once she left home she would call her mother in the fall: "Did you see the birds?" Her mother always did, and always thought of her. It connected them whether they were physically together or not.

Sonja's first bird art focused on the sparrow as a metaphor. She said, "It was a vehicle through which I could talk about my fear, coming to terms with the changes my mom's body was going through and then the grief after she died—the fear and sadness of watching the birds flying overheard alone. There was something sacred and poetic about the sparrow metaphor, almost shrine or relic-like." But, Sonja said, "it became more of a crutch over time and a way to avoid dealing with the underbelly of death."

Her dreams and artwork of the Chicken Lady pushed her to another level. The first birds were clean, sparrows, presentable, and sacred. Sonja says, "Chickens seemed so different than other birds: dirty and dumb and consumable. There is nothing poetic about a chicken."

Taking her cue from her dreams of Beulah, Sonja began dissecting chickens, which, she said, smelled surprisingly fresh, "like something that had just been living." We have all the same organs as a chicken, and Sonja said she was never so aware of her liver as when she took the bird's liver out—how it was all compact. It made her mother's cancer so much more understandable—it was the first time she'd really grasped what was going on in her body.

Some of Sonja's chicken work was installed at our church, House of Mercy. As liturgical art, it was haunting and tender. Sonja described the piece as an investigation of the book of Luke. She was thinking about the uninvited and the untouchables as well as her mother's disease. She began to think of the chicken as "the untouchable of the bird kingdom," but she also liked how much it is tied into daily life.

I recently visited the growing project that has become "Beulah's room" on the first floor of Sonja's house. The room gives the dream a visual representation, as Sonja creates artifacts of an imagined life. These include a curiosity cabinet full of quilted prayer cloths for Holy Week. Each day's prayer coincides with a station of the cross—illustrated with a different chicken part. Monday is the heart, representing the betrayal. Tuesday: Jesus stands before Pilate—the throat is cut. Thursday, Jesus takes his last breath—Beulah quilts the lungs. The room smells of spices. It is a comforting space—serene even in the face of dissected chicken parts and death.

On Passion Sunday, Sonja preached a sermon at our church called "How to Butcher a Chicken." In it she extended the story of the imagined world to Beulah as a little girl and Mike the Headless Chicken, a bird that survived a botched attempt at butchering and eventually achieved sideshow fame. Ultimately it was about Jesus. Sonja said,

> I'd like to focus on the resurrection and skim over the walk toward death. It would be easier. But I won't. Palm Sunday

signals the beginning of the end—Jesus walking toward the darkness. We have the birth of Jesus walking ahead of us and the resurrected Jesus approaching from behind us. And right now we are in the middle—we are walking alongside the crucified and dying Jesus. We are walking toward darkness. The sky will soon turn black when Jesus is on the cross. Our Savior will be strung up and bled out. In the Epistle reading for today we are called to be of the same mind as Jesus—we are called to become nothing, to be humbled and obedient to death—even death on a cross. Darkness is all around us—circling in on us—and I feel it. Darkness will be all we know. We all will be bled out and the ground will become dark and wet beneath our feet. When we meet again as a community it will be at the Stations of the Cross. With any luck the Stations will move beyond a memorial procession and we will participate in our own passion of being emptied out, bled out, and begin transcending. But there is no transcending, no resurrection without death. There is no purification without destruction. We can't know the light until we face the darkness. Grace still exists, even if the darkness covers it.

She went on to describe some videos she'd watched on how to butcher a chicken. She said, "Let's be honest. Death is always a struggle." But then at the last, she told a story of a young Beulah being held in her father's comforting arms while they watched a chicken being butchered: "The father whispers to her softly, secretly—so softly no one else can hear—he whispers, 'Beulah, look. Just look at that bird. Even though he's dying, he can't help but dance. Don't cry, sweet pea. Just stay here and watch that bird dance.'"

DOMESTICATION

One way to talk about domestication is to say that we have turned wild beasts into animals we can live with and rely on—it's a process where humans change animals at a genetic level, selecting for the traits they desire. But in some cases, domestication may be more of a two-way street. Wild wolves benefited from being near humans. They were attracted to refuse left at human campsites. The least fearful and most social wolves passed on these traits, eventually resulting in animals that were more and more comfortable being near us until, finally, we had the dog. So, you could say, wolves chose to be domesticated at some level.

Some say the chicken's life today is worse than it's ever been. Although some domestic poultry are still allowed to roam freely around the yard or farmstead, many are now intensely farmed by factory methods meant to maximize economic returns without concern for the bird's quality of life, to put it mildly. They live in row upon row of cages where they barely have room to move. They can hardly be said to have a real life—they are eating-and-laying machines. Conveyor belts carry eggs away as soon as they are laid. Broilers are fattened and killed within five weeks of being born.

Of course Jesus did not intend to compare himself to a factory-farmed chicken, but it is still a strange bird to call to mind. Maybe the story of Jesus is like the story of a God who will let himself be domesticated—a God who chooses it. It is a very strange story. Jesus was a placental mammal, a higher vertebrate. I thought about this at dinner one night as my mammal family was gnashing a dead mammal between their four types of well-developed mammal teeth. "Jesus was a mammal," I said. "What does that mean?" Olivia, having recently covered this in biology, said, "It means he was covered with fur except on his lips." God became a hairy four-limbed animal with a face and toes that have nails. Our God found this to be an essential way of revealing Godself to us.

God incarnate dribbled his mother's milk out of his mouth. Spit up. Had three bones in his inner ear, one in the jaw; gas, bacteria. God incarnate, sucking at his mother's breast, lying on her lap, unable to hold his own head up, so she cradles it in her hands. God incarnate at thirteen: finding that hair is growing in his armpits. God incarnate: enzymes breaking down molecules so they can be absorbed by his intestines. It is strange.

The Incarnation has been hard for people to deal with from day one. The religious authorities wanted to kill the incarnate God almost immediately—the charge was blasphemy. Jesus blasphemes in his very being. How could he, this man—all whiskers and toenails and wine breath, his hands all filthy with the sweat of the untouchables, the lepers—be the Messiah, the Son of God, so unholy that the religious enterprise wanted to kill him to protect the faith. The body of Christ messes with the divisions of the sacred and the profane. The divine inhabits flesh (saliva, semen, and excrement). And maybe if we're going to know Jesus, we ought to feel the tension that the collapse of the boundaries creates.

God allows Godself to be domesticated—chooses it to be near to us. In this he lays himself open to the possibility of endless misinterpretation. Think of Warner Sallman's *Head of*

Christ. I'm sure you've seen it. Sallman was an ad man (and a sincere and devout Christian). He created the picture under deadline one night as part of a product line made for mass consumption—for the cover of a magazine. Sallman's assignment was to give Christ a new image, to refashion Christ for the modern age—which at the time, was all about linking therapeutic religiosity with an ideology of consumption. The portrait was made to be marketable, to fulfill the main objective of modern advertising—to move merchandise to as many consumers as possible. It has been reproduced more than five hundred million times—as calendar art, cheap posters; it was pasted on Sunday school rewards and clocks. Many people interviewed in a book on Sallman's art, *The Icons of American Protestantism,* said they considered it to be an accurate representation of Jesus. I'm embarrassed to write this, but I don't think it's an accident that I fell in love with and married a man who bears some resemblance to Sallman's head of Jesus. This image, meant to appeal to and not challenge consumer desire, monopolized many people's imaginations.

It seems that all this might humiliate any god with dignity. Maybe God gave up God's dignity in Jesus Christ because what is most important to God is to be with us, close to us—maybe this is actually essential to God's nature in some way that is more pressing than God's grandeur. To become incarnate in the world is to lay oneself open to mistreatment, all the distorting arenas of interpretation and misinterpretation—more so than if one has always kept one's distance, remaining above the fray. God becomes something we can get our hands on. I'm not sure it's a move that quite creates reverence—it seems that God might have been going for something else—something closer and deeper.

Sometimes we understand the profundity of God's move in the Incarnation. Other times we drain the blood, remove the bones, wrap Jesus in plastic, and sell him. It's surprising that God would make Godself vulnerable to us in this way. We are not necessarily 100 percent reliable. But this is what love is like—relationship. It's more about becoming vulnerable than taking power, or controlling.

CHICKEN JESUS

In Christian art, Jesus is represented more often as a lion or an eagle than a hen, even though he himself gives us the image: Jesus as chicken. Did the church veer away from this representation from the beginning because it was too emasculating? However Jesus thought of himself, or the revelation of God he embodied (receive a child and you receive me and my Father who sent me), we'd like to think of him as big and strong and awesomely powerful—never quite embracing that he sought to upend our notions of the powerful. Jesus is sometimes identified with the ox, domesticated but sturdy. But the lamb—the lamb is everywhere.

Christ does not come in power. This is a truth so deeply embedded in our narratives of him that it is hard to get away from—no matter how we might try. He comes as a baby. He is baptized by John. He heals some people, but he doesn't even come close to being as effective as the smallpox vaccine. Yes, he says at one point that he came to bring a sword, but he doesn't bring one literally at all. These weren't the words of a violent man. He wasn't talking about waging holy war; he was talking about what the effect of following him might be. Converting to the truth of the gospel of a suffering Savior might cause some rifts within your family, with the structures put in place by a more normal sort of society. Moments after he mentions the sword, he praises "whoever gives to one of these little ones even a cup of cold water." Jesus doesn't dine with the emperor, or slay dragons. His work in the world may be something closer to setting out little bowls of water to keep the sparrows from dying of thirst.

Jesus doesn't make many power plays. And yet we seem to persistently try to somehow skew the story in the direction of power. We seem to desperately want to believe in a powerful god. We want astonishing displays of power. I do. But as far as I know—as far as I can tell so far, God doesn't act this way. Love doesn't keep people from suffering. I know that. I'm not sure how we could trust or love an almighty God who doesn't use almightiness to do something to keep little babies in Rwanda from being hacked to death with machetes. It is understandable that we want a powerful God, but I'm not sure that desire really leads us to more truth, or more goodness, or a better world.

The Roman Empire was mighty and it claimed to serve its citizens, but in the end it didn't really serve the poor. When Constantine made Christianity the religion of empire, there may have been a few humane results, but you can't possibly look at the Crusades and the Inquisition and the conquistadores and not question the attempt to merge conventional power with the gospel.

Jürgen Moltmann, a theologian who has emphasized the fact that God suffers, writes, "If Christ is weak and humble on earth, then God is weak and humble in heaven." I don't think that's usually how we think of God. The Christian church is distinct from other communities of faith because it believes that God revealed Godself most fully in Jesus Christ. Believing in Jesus is different from believing in the Almighty. However much we might want an Almighty, I don't think that's what we get in God. Indeed, to be a creator involves some sort of power, but creative power seems very different to me than might.

Much of the world worships THE ALMIGHTY, if not a powerful, all-knowing deity, then just power. It's like the default move. Power rules. What else would make God, God? Isn't that practically what "God" means—some magisterial, omnipotent, almighty protector?

The almighty God is distant, and when you get down to it, sort of noncommunicative—certainly not very verbal. This is not the God of the Old Testament, who is feeling and even at times loquacious, or the God of the New Testament, but it does seem to be the God of the popular imagination—the God of the universe. In *A Gentler God,* Doug Frank suggests that Jesus wants his followers to see that they have a sort of self-destructive allegiance to a big strong distant unknowable unsatisfying god. Jesus says, "Receive me." I don't think this is a ploy to gain power; it reveals the desire of a God who wants to be close to us.

Phyllis recently returned to the church after a forty-five-year sojourn, during which she lived according to Christ's teaching, providing therapy for the underprivileged and abused, speaking truth to power, but could not bear to align herself under Christ's name. This is because she was abused by a powerful Christian father and because she couldn't bear the rhetoric of some of the more belligerently patriarchal Christian elements. I was so happy to hear her preach in church last Sunday. She spoke about the text that comes after Jesus teaches about his flesh and blood in John. The Scripture said these were hard sayings, and many disciples drew back and no longer went about with him. Jesus looked at the Twelve and said, "Do you also want to leave?" This seemed so vulnerable to Phyllis—so unlike the God who needs nothing, so almighty is he, and it opened her heart to him.

"Receive me," Jesus pleads. Jesus asks us to *receive* him. This is so different from a king demanding his subjects to bow down. God reveals Godself in the crucified Christ. Look at him. His hands are tied. Luther said if we don't look first at the crucified Christ to see God, we are making friends with the devil: the power of the world. Of course, we may want to make friends with the power of the world. It makes it much easier to live under its reign. What Luther saw, though, is that the God who hangs on the gallows crushed by the madness of human history is the only god that can help us.

If you look at Jesus with the idea that looking at him will tell you what God is like, God isn't about showing us how great God is. God's thing isn't power. Like, really isn't, not just like it could be but it isn't. God's thing is not anything like what we know of as power; or the kind of power we crave, or believe in, or follow, or try to have. It's the power in the blood of the lamb—the little lamby, the puny baby sheep. What kind of wonder-working power does that blood have? Seems like it's a whole different sort of thing than punching anything in the face. Frank says that perhaps "God simply does not have the kind of power we ourselves crave." Maybe we made up the Almighty, the all-powerful, because it's what we think we want, but it's not really what we need.

What we need is love. All the posturing, the power-grabbing, the diminishing other people to make ourselves great—maybe it's because we want to be loved. It seems true to me. Jesus reveals God's essential being: not power—but love. Imagine God as a hen with her wings over her babies. That is not the same as a concrete bunker. There is some fragility in it. Maybe there's something crucial about that, which we lose when we keep imagining it's all in the hands of an almighty God. It's different to imagine it under the wings of a chicken.

We're all actually sort of semifragile people. A little itty-bitty virus could kill us, and Mike Tyson, too. There are black holes out there. We are small, like children who need to be loved. We could spend our lives involved in some destructive life-sucking game to try to prove otherwise, or maybe we could relax into what might save us from our violence-spawning fears and hate-making anxiety.

We desire love. God is trying to get through to us that we are given love. We actually don't even need to strive for it; it's running through us. We want love, we need it, we long for it. We have it—in some unimaginably thorough way. But try to imagine it. Wouldn't it be a relief to know it—to feel like you could just be who you are: weak or cocky; patriotic, unpatriotic; common, uncommon; terribly fragile in moments, strong in others—a human being held in love.

When Jesus breaks his body and pours out his blood, he's feeding us God's essential love. He fed it to Peter and Judas and all the disciples. It's hard to believe that he placed it in their hands and in their mouths. It's hard to believe he places it in ours. We neglect it, or fail to see it, or don't handle it very well; but if all we ever do is love some little thing, it will be godlike.

THE
RAVEN

FAILURE *and* TRUST

THERE ARE DEAD MICE on our doorsteps many mornings, dehydrated frogs along the gravel road, dead deer on the highway, flattened snakes on the grass, and I am not greatly disturbed. But when I hear the thunk of a bird smashing against the glass in my kitchen window, my heart races. I feel through my entire body that something terrible has happened. A bird colliding with a window seems catastrophic.

These little beings, this life-form, can take flight, defy gravity, soar, and migrate south two thousand miles to warmer climates without burning an ounce of fossil fuel, without maps or compasses. In the ancient mythologies of almost every culture, birds represent more than what we see: the soul, the dead reborn, higher states of consciousness, resurrection—they are messengers of the gods. Perhaps because somewhere in our collective unconscious they represent the "more" of hope, when they collide with our windows and fall to the ground, it feels devastating.

When three thousand birds fell from the sky in Arkansas on New Year's Eve, residents believed it must be the end of the world. I understand.

In the Gospels, Jesus asks his hearers to "consider the birds." This is something that has come naturally to humans throughout the ages. We feed them, watch them, and invest them with meaning. "Look at the birds in the sky," Matthew writes. This sounds like a delightful, if at times heartbreaking, directive—easier than selling all that you have to give to the poor, than offering your body as a living sacrifice or loving your enemy; less unwieldy than putting on the whole armor of God (whatever that means). Birds are not held by the weighty burdens of the earth.

In Luke's Gospel, Jesus' words are slightly different. The directive takes on a different shade. Jesus says, "Consider the ravens." Matthew's "birds of the air" seem light and sweet somehow; look at the colorful things flittering and chirping and singing, all little and cute. Considering the raven is a different affair. Ravens don't often fly into windows, and if they did it would be more frightening than heartbreaking. They don't evoke our protective instincts. Children don't pick up dazed ravens and feed them with medicine droppers, keep them in a box, stroke their feathers.

Ravens are big (up to 27 inches long and 3.6 pounds) and they are black (their entire body, bills, legs, feet—the raven's eyes even look black) and they are ugly (depending on how you see things). The raven has shaggy throat hackles, pointy feathers that stick out around its neck. It has prominent nasal bristles. It doesn't sing, it croaks—a hollow honk, a dry grating *kraa,* low guttural rattles.

People describing the raven's voice often say, "It sounds like death." Consider the raven. Seriously, consider it.

"Cute" and "sweet" don't describe it well. I got out all my bird books. First I looked at the yellow warbler (cute, sweet); then I considered the raven. I showed the photo of the raven to Miles, my son. "Miles," I said, "what do you think of the raven?" He said, "Menacing." People across time and place have believed the raven to be an omen of death. In some cultures people believed the raven could smell death coming and would hover over the place where a person was going to die. It has represented war and destruction, doom, the void, annihilation, death. The bird, to put it mildly, invokes anxiety. When Jesus says, "Don't be anxious. Consider the raven," is he joking? Or is he saying something like "Look straight into the black abyss of death and fear not"? When Jesus says, "Consider the raven," is he saying something more than "Get out your binoculars and take a stroll"? Perhaps he is saying something more (it wouldn't be unlike him).

SINNER BIRD

Maybe Jesus didn't mean to be tapping into anything dark, or Luke didn't mean to be saying anything weighty when he changed Matthew's little chirpy birds of the air into the raven, but the raven has a significant presence in the text. In the book of Proverbs, we meet ravens plucking out the eyes of disobedient children. In the prophetic writings of Isaiah, ravens haunt the ruins of a civilization laid waste by the wrath of God—along with the stench of corpses, the rot, the thorns, and the jackals.

Why bring the raven into a discourse meant to free its hearers from anxiety?

The raven is the first bird to be referred to by name in the Bible—in the story of Noah's ark (eighth chapter of the first book, actually). We all know about the dove that Noah sent out of the ark to see if there was dry land, but before he sent the dove, he opened the window of the ark and released a raven. The text doesn't say why, exactly, the raven was released, though a purpose was assigned to the dove. And you wouldn't believe the amount of biblical commentary devoted to this ambiguity: why the raven? What was the purpose? Is it a textual error, a missing story?

Not a few scholars have taken the whole thing to mean that the raven failed. Clearly its purpose was meant to be the same as the dove's (to see if the waters had receded), but the raven's mission failed. In some ancient Jewish commentary, the raven was originally white (pure and pretty), but its feathers were turned black as a curse on its species when it failed to return to the ark. A lot of cultures have told similar stories about how the raven started out white but was turned black because of some transgression. Like Hester Prynne, marked with her scarlet letter, the raven's body was marked with this emblem of shame, splayed out, for all to see.

The raven failed. It failed and so it was turned black. It was condemned to be the hated, dark, bad, sinner bird. So then Noah sent out the dove—the lovely little cooing snow-white dove, pure sweet love, who comes back with the olive branch. So the dove becomes the symbol of the good and the beautiful—peace and love and the Holy Spirit; and the raven, in the collective unconscious, in Christian symbolism, in myriad mythologies, becomes the symbol of evil.

The church, with all its beauty, does tend to occasionally revel in this sort of binary thinking: making something a symbol of depravity and then digging in. The raven is perhaps a bit unduly maligned. Early Christian commentators frequently comment on the raven's failure: it found corpses killed by the Flood, and because it is a filthy carrion eater, distracted by its appetite (the evil beast), it became preoccupied by the corpses. It eats flesh and blood (never mind that we do, too), and so it failed Noah. It failed God, really. It was bad. Philo, the Jewish commentator received most enthusiastically by the early Christians, looked at the nonreturn of the raven to the ark and pronounced it the symbol of Satan. He said the raven is "arrogant and shamelessly impudent," so that in expelling the raven from the ark, Noah was expelling "whatever residue of darkness there was in the mind which might have led to folly."

But, in fact, the residue remains. There seems to be lots of residue left that leads to folly. All over the place. In my mind, in the Senate, in Rome and South Dakota, all over the advertising industry. Augustine said the raven personified impure men and "procrastinators." It's a bird. It's an animal. It does what it does because it is what it is. Funny, how easily we're aroused in condemnation. The raven is black. It has a different diet than the dove. But is the dove really somehow more innocent? And if so, what good is innocence, if it is merely prescribed by genetic material?

MIXING

The enduring beauty of the Bible is due in part to its tendency to deconstruct itself. Reading Joshua, the Canaanites are made out to be the evil, faithless enemy. Later on, though, Jesus offers an amazing reversal to the Canaanite woman when he says, "How great is your faith!" Narratives of triumph are duly undermined. The betrayers drink wine with the betrayed. What is condemned in the text is very frequently redeemed in the text at a later time or different place. Maybe this redemption is even for the birds. Maybe the Word of God keeps rolling with grace so thick and unrelenting—it's even for the raven. Jesus says, "Consider the raven": God cares for this condemned and hated carrion-eating procrastinator. God makes sure it is fed. God is an indiscriminating feeder—of course, God will care for you. Innocence is not a prerequisite.

The ancient rabbis talk about the ravens a lot, and as is so often the case with the rabbis, they don't speak of the raven in black-and-white terms. They say that ravens are a mixture. Even their name in Hebrew is similar to the word for "mixture." They are the only bird to have two of the signs of kosher birds and two of the signs of nonkosher birds. The Midrash notes that the raven also has a tendency to mix even when mixing is forbidden. According to the midrashic view, there was no intercourse allowed on Noah's ark—no mixing was permitted on the ark. But "there were three that engaged in sexual relations while in the ark: Ham, the raven, and the dog." What a curious character, that raven.

A mix seems right. In the sacred narratives of Native

Americans, the raven appears sometimes as creator, sometimes trickster. Shamans say the raven is an ideal guide on the path of the deepest mysteries (attach a raven feather to a dream catcher and hang it over your bed). Yet anyone who observes the raven for long recognizes its remarkable capacity for deception. They work in teams. One will distract the mark, a feeding hawk or fox, while the other darts in from behind and steals its meal. Scientists marvel at the raven's ability to fool other birds with elaborate performances—faking injury, distracting drama, conning competition out of food or resources. They seem to be opportunists living by their wits. Yet ravens will share resources, not just with their own, but with other species. Their relationship with wolves is well attested. Ravens follow hunting packs and share their kills. Barry Lopez, in his book *Of Wolves and Men,* says, "The wolf seems to have few relationships with other animals that could be termed purely social, though he apparently takes pleasure in the company of ravens."

Although they are often called accomplished liars and thieves, they are devoted parents and they mate for life. One study determined that they fall in love. They perform spectacular courtship flights where they fly and swoop—do corkscrews, barrel rolls, plummeting dives; wing tip to wing tip, they lock talons as they tumble through the sky in sheer exuberance. They don't build storehouses or barns. Ravens have been seen sliding down snow-covered hills, apparently, just for fun. Bernd Heinrich (an internationally known biologist), in his book *The Mind of the Raven,* describes watching ravens listen intently for over two hours to men playing guitars.

In the Hebrides they say giving a child his first drink from the skull of a raven will give the child powers of prophecy and wisdom. I like considering the raven.

The raven has a prominent place in Celtic, Ukrainian, Brahman, Shinto, Inuit, Cherokee, Wiccan, and Norse legend. Two ravens, named Hugin (thought) and Munin (memory), sat on the Norse god Odin's shoulders, so the story goes. They would fly out all over the world, hungrily gathering news and wisdom, returning to their perch to whisper the knowledge into Odin's ear. Dwarfs who lived on the slopes of Kilimanjaro supposedly laid out bits of meat in banana groves when sacrificing to their ancestors. Later, when these bits of meat rolled down the slopes, they turned into ravens. In Japanese mythologies, supernatural beings with the head and wings of a raven serve fallen monks: tall men with big noses and red faces who can create tornadoes using fans of raven feathers they carry in their sandals. The raven has some great anecdotes to tell at the bird feeder.

Scientists widely agree that the raven is the smartest bird there is. A raven's brain is as large in relationship to its body as a chimpanzee's. They share the cognitive capacities of primates. Not only can they use tools, they can make tools. Captive ravens have even been taught to speak.

In the Midrash the raven speaks eloquently, displaying its intellectual acumen in a verbal dispute with Noah. The rabbis playfully re-create the dialogue, suggesting that the raven didn't fly off in pursuit of dry land, but stayed around the ark because it was concerned with the preservation of its species. Noah sent it on his mission, but, Rabbi Resh Lakis says, "the raven retorts to Noah with a winning argument." The raven knew if he left the ark and for some reason couldn't get back, there would be only one raven left in the world without any other raven to mate with, and the species would die out. The raven says, "Should the master of heat or the master of cold attack me, will not the world be short of one type of creature?" Other rabbis suggest the raven wouldn't go on Noah's mission because it didn't trust him—because it believed, actually, that Noah had designs on its mate.

CONSIDER THE SIMILARITIES

The raven is smart; it's wily and adaptable. It likes to eat flesh and have sex. It seems to me that the raven is not entirely unlike us. Some ornithologists have reached similar conclusions. With its big brain and its cognitive capacities, they say, consider the similarities. We are both highly social species, adapt readily to changes in environmental conditions. We are both generalists and opportunists about food and can exploit a huge variety of resources.

The raven is a mixture. But in Leviticus it is classified as unclean, an abomination. One theory purports that it is considered unclean because of its morose and solitary lifestyle (for bats—it's their hypocrisy and double life. For owls—it's their love of darkness). But a little later on in the text, it's the raven that flies into the desert where Elijah is stranded, "and the ravens brought him bread and meat in the morning, and bread and meat in the evening." What is condemned one place in the text is redeemed in another. The raven may have failed Noah, but he fed the great prophet Elijah for days, enabling him to survive the desert.

Nevertheless, negative feelings persist. Humans often have strong feelings about the Corvidae family in general (crows, jays, magpies, ravens). They are called dirty, destructive, aggressive, greedy, gluttonous, and mean. They have been poisoned, trapped, and shot. They are hated because they eat the flesh of the bodies that lie dead in our battlefields and because they scavenge our Dumpsters and fast-food debris. Some anthropologists have theorized that primitive humans may have learned to cooperate with one another as a way to defend their kills against scavenger ravens. They suggest our species may have coevolved somehow. Perhaps this explains some of our lingering antagonism. The raven became the scapegoat, the scape*bird*—the enemy on whom we might project the darkness so that we could bond with one another.

And yet, they have been called gods, creators, wisdom, and memory. The only constancy of the raven, according to one writer who has cataloged its symbolism and mythology, is its quest to fulfill its appetite—whether it's hungry for food or prophecy, friendship or the spirits of the dead, healing or the love of its mate, the appetite is always there, strong and determinative.

DON'T BE ANXIOUS

The raven is a creature of need, of want, of desire. It is voracious. And God feeds it, takes care of its needs, so Jesus would have us believe. Jesus tells us to consider this bird to help relieve ourselves of our anxieties about life, about food, about clothing and money. Don't be anxious. Consider the raven: the complex, paradoxical, voracious little embodiment of life. Consider the raven.

Ravens are friends with wolves. They are acrobats. They dance. The book of Job suggests that it is God who feeds their young when they cry, thus they have often been accused of being bad mothers. Could there be anything more shameful? They are scavengers. They are ravenous. They rave. They mix—when mixing is not allowed. They are creatures of paradox and God feeds them. Jesus says, "Don't be anxious, consider the raven"—the raven is not unburdened by the weight of the world (perhaps its brain is too big); it carries it around on its big black wings. You can see the dark in its eyes. And God feeds it.

It's one thing to believe God feeds the little pretty birds of the air. They have small appetites. They need a few seeds. Everybody loves them. It's not that much to feed. They do not seem needy. But what if you're ravenous?

Is the hope that God will feed you as long as you're not that hungry, as long as you don't need that much? God will feed you, sure—if you have the appetite of a little dove, as long as all you need is seeds, dry little seeds? The hope is not so proscribed.

God feeds the ravens, the ravenous, the mixed-up greedy glutton carrion eater. That's saying a lot more, somehow—something more shocking, maybe, than that God's willing to give bird food to light eaters. And how much more will God feed us? We need a lot. A lot of food and attention and love and healing. The world needs a lot. And I don't think I usually believe that God will feed us all. Jesus seems crazy here to me, unreliable, like, how can we even listen to him here? How can we model ourselves on the raven, the lilies—it's lunacy to ask us to believe we will be fed.

What if we could trust that we will be fed? Maybe that's the most important thing we could ever know fewer. And somehow if we knew it, a lot more people would get fed and a lot fewer people would be left hopeless in the wake of our schemes and dramas and deceits. What if God feeds our children in some way we're not capable of, even when we fail them? What if we could trust God? To let not even the raven go, much less the world?

ACKNOWLEDGMENTS

Of course I am indebted to a world of thinkers, but there are several writers and theologians whose ideas surface all over these pages. I learned to question the idea of sacrifice from James Alison—from his book *Raising Abel,* as well as his lectures at House of Mercy. His ideas about desire and about Peter's heart breaking are essential to what I have written. I studied Avivah Gottlieb Zornberg's *The Particulars of Rapture* and *The Murmuring Deep* to learn about the quail story and the Israelites wandering in the wilderness, Moses, and Mount Sinai. Her ideas are present in the quail chapter. I was guided throughout by Doug Frank's book *A Gentler God*. He articulates, far more eloquently and thoroughly than I was able, reason to question the concept of an almighty God. I highly recommend all these books to you. I never would have been interested in the Bible if it weren't for Jon Linton. His ideas are reflected everywhere in this book.

I am grateful to my friend and neighbor Linda Buturian for reading my chapters and helping to shape them. Rev. Russell Rathbun, my colleague at the House of Mercy, supported the idea for this book from the beginning. Many of my thoughts on the text come out of conversations with him. Brett and Diane, bird experts and farm mates, talked to me about birds and let me use them as foils for the sparrow chapter. Sonja Olson is the artist who created Beulah. I have benefited from her chicken-inspired art over the last ten years. I'm grateful to Lil Copan for helping to develop the idea for a book about the birds of the Bible; and to Lauren Winner for talking me through what worked and what didn't work so well. The book benefited greatly from the work of these two outstanding editors, as well as the beautiful illustrations by my husband, Jim. Thanks to the House of Mercy community for giving me time off to write and for so very many other things; and to my family—Jim, Miles, and Olivia—for sustaining me.

NOTES

Introduction
Whereas many translations use the phrase "look at the birds," I chose the phrasing from the Lexham English Bible. This phrase suits my purposes more. People *look at* birds every day. I want us to *consider* them.

"Hope is the thing with feathers."
Dickinson: Collected Poems and Commentaries, ed. Helen Vendler (Cambridge, MA: Harvard University Press, 2010), 118.

1. The Pigeon—Purity and Impurity
"Let birds fly," and "Let the birds multiply."
Genesis 1:20, 22

"The Spirit of God hovered over the surface of the waters—like a dove."
Twelfth Tractate Hagiga (The Festival Sacrifices). See *The Talmud: A Selection,* trans. Norman Solomon (London: Penguin, 2009), 293.

"This is my son in whom I am well pleased."
Matthew 3:17 NRSV

"I saw the Spirit . . . remained on him."
John 1:32 RSV

"Little scrawny blue and white, messenger for men who fight."
Harry Webb Farrington, *Cher Ami* (New York: Rough and Brown Press, 1926), 14.

"and that believing you may have life."
John 20:31 RSV

"always take cruel delight in knocking down the little birds."
Charles Darwin, *The Voyage of the Beagle* (Amherst, N.Y.: Prometheus Books, 2000), 422.

Gilgamesh says, "Listen to me . . . his own hounds worry his flanks."
The Epic of Gilgamesh, trans. N. K. Sandars (London: Penguin, 1985), 86.

"bring up the dead to eat the living."
Morris Jastrow, *Descent of the Goddess Ishtar into the Lower World* (Charles River Editors, 2012).

Pigeons are known for their sexual appetite.
I learned many wonderful things about pigeons from Andrew D. Blechman, *Pigeons: The Fascinating Saga of the World's Most Revered and Reviled Bird* (New York: Grove Press, 2006). You may find reference to their appetites throughout his book.

"infinite multitudes," "countless numbers."
Bob Dylan's *Theme Time Radio Hour,* episode 71, "Birds." Aired on March 5, 2008.

"She did not permit . . . modest and compassionate."
Moshe Bogomilsky, "Shemini Q&A," on Chabad.org, accessed September 23, 2011, www.chabad.org/parshah/article_cdo/aid/375920/jewish/Shemini-Q-A.htm.

"Torah chose animals...take weapons against."
Kabbalah Online, trans. Rahmiel-Hayyim Drizon, accessed September 25, 2011, www.chabad.org/kabbalah/article_cdo/aid/1456132/jewish/Loyal-Pigeons-and-Devoted-Doves.htm.

"shall bring his offering . . . for ashes."
Leviticus 1:14-16 RSV

"Start with the birth itself . . . The womb."
Tertullian, *On the Flesh of Christ,* quoted in a blog by David Lose, "Preaching the Scandal and the Glory of the Incarnation," on Working Preacher.org, accessed December 19, 2010, www.workingpreacher.org/theologypreaching.aspx?article, Dec. 11, 2007.

"There is no such thing as absolute dirt . . . the beholder."
Mary Douglas, *Purity and Danger: An Analysis of Concepts of Pollution and Taboo* (London: Routledge, 2002), 2.

"Imagine the complications . . . Chagga men."
Douglas, *Purity and Danger,* 201.

2. The Pelican—Sacrifice and Gift
The YouTube pelican video with by far the most hits . . . pigeon whole.
To see this pelican video, go to www.youtube.com/watch?v=je9NARZJJwg.

"O loving Pelican! O Jesu Lord!"
The lines are found in "Adoro Te Devote," a hymn composed by Thomas Aquinas in 1264. The hymn is found in the Roman Missal as a prayer of Thanksgiving after Mass.

Dante and Shakespeare use the image as well: Jesus Christ our Pelican.
Dante refers to the pelican in the "Paradiso" of his *Divine Comedy.* Shakespeare refers to it in *Hamlet.*

"He wasn't trying to eat the baby ducks. Pelicans are just jerks."
The YouTube video of the pelican chasing the ducks can be found at
www.youtube.com/watch?v=dIJk0w4SnH8.

"Perching pelicans are the ugliest birds imaginable...Levitical abominations."
Gene Stratton-Porter, "Pelicans," in *International Standard Bible Encyclopedia*
(Grand Rapids: Eerdmans, 1939).

"Ask the beasts...declare to you."
Job 12:7-8 RSV

"Consider the birds."
See Matthew 6:26. The CEB version reads "Look at the birds in the sky."

"understand that thou hast within thyself...within thee."
Origen, *The Fathers of the Church Series: Homilies on Leviticus,* trans. Gary
Wayne Barkley (Washington, DC: Catholic University of America Press,
1990), 91–92.

Aristotle wrote one of the first... (after which...are modeled).
For all the quotations that follow, see Aristotle, *The History of Animals,* bk. 1,
trans. D'Arcy Wentworth Thompson, accessed November 8, 2011, http://
classics.mit.edu/Aristotle/history_anim.1.i.html.

"In the same way, our Lord Jesus Christ."
The Book of Beasts, a twelfth-century manuscript, can be found at University of
Wisconsin Digital Collections, accessed November 8, 2011, http://digital
.library.wisc.edu/1711.dl/HistSciTech.Bestiary 132,133.

Yet most people believe deeply in the sacred character of sacrifice.
I have been deeply influenced by Rene Girard, by way of James Alison, on the
nature of sacrifice. All of James Alison's books deal with this, but see especially
Raising Abel: The Recovery of the Eschatological Imagination (New York:
Crossroad, 2003).

"the sacrifices borne by our ancestors."
Obama's inaugural address (2009) can be found at Inspire Political Discourse,
accessed December 12, 2012, http://indiedesign.typepad.com/inspire_
political_discour/2009/01/full-transcript-of-president-obamas-inaugural
-speech.html.

God does not desire our sacrifice.
See, for example, 1 Samuel 15:22; Psalms 40:6; 51:16; Hosea 6:6.

"I want mercy and not sacrifice."
See Matthew 12:7.

"Go and learn what this means. 'I desire...not sacrifice.'"
Matthew 9:13 RSV

"This is my body, which is given for you."
Luke 22:19

3. The Quail—Desire and Slavery

"until it comes out of your nostrils."
Numbers: 11:20

"a day's journey."
Numbers 11:31

"while the meat was still between their teeth."
Numbers 11:33

Augustine believed . . . inordinate desire.
Augustine, *Confessions.*

"bread of the angels."
Psalm 78:25 RSV

"bread from heaven."
Nehemiah 9:15; John 6:31

"their own desire."
Psalm 78:29 KJV

On Cyprus the illegal dish . . . with little birds.
I learned these terms reading Jonathan Franzen's story "Emptying the Skies," *New Yorker* (July 26, 2010): 48–61.

"a massive database . . . across the world."
Encyclopedia of Life, accessed November 22, 2011, http://eol.org/info/"
the_history_of_eol.

"pet trade / food."
"Coturnix Coturnix—Details," *Encyclopedia of Life.*

"People ask me . . . is all one."
M. F. K. Fisher, *The Art of Eating* (Hoboken: Wiley, 2004), 353.

"Taste and see how good the LORD is!"
Psalm 34:8

"My whole being thirsts for God."
Psalm 42:2

"Your word is so pleasing to my taste buds."
Psalm 119:103

"Hearken diligently to me, and eat what is good, and delight yourselves in fatness."
Isaiah 55:2 RSV

"Whoever comes to me will never go hungry."
John 6:35

"child still at the breast . . . cometh from the Lord."
Saint Francis de Sales, quoted in Kim Chernin, *The Hungry Self: Women, Eating, and Identity* (New York: Random House), 198.

They struggle repeatedly with this insecurity.
I have relied heavily upon Avivah Gottlieb Zornberg's reading of the quail story and the Israelites' wandering in the wilderness, Moses, and Mount Sinai. See Zornberg, *The Particulars of Rapture: Reflections on Exodus* (New York: Doubleday, 2002); and Zornberg, *The Murmuring Deep: Reflections on the Biblical Unconscious* (New York: Schocken, 2009).

"Is it because . . . wilderness?"
Exodus 14:11 RSV

"Would that we . . . with hunger."
Exodus 16:3 RSV

"Behold, I will rain bread from heaven."
Exodus 16:4 RSV

"I have heard . . . your God."
Exodus 16:12 RSV

"became infested with worms and stank."
Exodus 16:20

"[God] gave them their own desire."
Psalm 78:29 KJV

"cakes baked in olive oil."
Numbers 11:8

From this they concluded . . . macaroni and cheese.
Midrash Tanchuma (Parshat B'Shalach 22).

"Pliny writes of their coming into Italy in such numbers . . . not appear incredible."
Gene Stratton-Porter, "Quail," *Bible Encyclopedia,* accessed June 17, 2013, http://classic.net.bible.org/dictionary.php?word=Quail.

"the casualty of thunder"
Gerrit Bos and Tzvi Langermann, "Pseudo Galen Al-Adwiya Al-Maktuma, with Commentary of Hunayn," Academia.edu, accessed November 14, 2011, www.academia.edu/1883273/Pseudo-Galen_al-Adwiya_al-Maktuma_with_commentary_of_Hunayn.

"If the cruel person eats from the heart of this bird . . . into friendliness."
Bos and Langermann, "Pseudo Galen."

Newly married couples in Lithuania... life together.
James Hastings, "Quail," *Encyclopedia of Religion and Ethics* (Edinburgh: T&T Clark, 1908), 525.

In other cultures... change into rats.
Hope B. Werness, "Quail," *The Continuum Encyclopedia of Animal Symbolism in Art* (New York: Continuum, 2004).

"stiff-necked."
Exodus 32:9; 33:3, 5; 34:9 RSV

they are too loose, fickle, inconstant, easily infatuated, and impatient.
See Zornberg, *Particulars of Rapture,* chap. 9, "Ki Tissa."

"Why... are you angry with the people you freed?"
See Exodus 32:11. The exact translation in the CEB version is "LORD, why does your fury burn against your own people, whom you brought out of the land of Egypt with great power and amazing force?"

"If this were not written in the text, it would be impossible."
Rabbi Abbahu, quoted in Zornberg, *Particulars of Rapture,* 414.

"Did I conceive... all these people?"
Numbers 11:12-13

"If this is how... please kill me."
See Numbers 11:15.

"The LORD will give you meat... who is among you."
Numbers 11:18-20 RSV

"the grave of craving."
See Numbers 11:34; *Kibroth-hattaavah* means "the grave of craving."

"we are being given imagination. Trust this."
James Alison, from my notes of the retreat he led for House of Mercy, May 2005.

4. The Vulture—Ugliness and Beauty
"Your dead body... birds of the air."
Deuteronomy 28:26 RSV

"Come to me... the birds."
1 Samuel 17:44 RSV

"Set the trumpet... of the LORD."
Hosea 8:1 RSV

"Wherever the corpse is... will gather."
Matthew 24:28 NRSV

"vulture of sedition."
William Shakespeare, *King Henry VI,* part 1.

"the gnawing vulture of thy mind."
William Shakespeare, *Titus Andronicus.*

"Mother of Mothers who existed ... to all that is."
Jenny Hill, "Nekhbet," in *Gods of Ancient Egypt,* accessed January 3, 2012, http://ancientegyptonline.co.uk/nekhbet.html%20.

"What can they say, those who ... denied as possible for vultures."
Aberdeen Bestiary, folio 44v, accessed January 4, 2012, www.abdn.ac.uk/bestiary/translat/44v.hti.

"You have seen ... to myself."
Exodus 19:4 RSV

"Like [a vulture] that stirs up its nest ... the LORD alone did lead him."
Deuteronomy 32:11-12 RSV

"Bless the LORD, O my soul ... like the [vulture's]."
Psalm 103:1-5 RSV

"Three things are too wonderful ... a man with a maiden."
Proverbs 30:18-19 RSV

"They who wait ... and not faint."
Isaiah 40:31 RSV

In 1973 a griffon vulture collided ... ever recorded for a bird.
Nosson Slifkin, "The Identity of the Nesher," in *Judaism and the Animal Kingdom,* accessed January 12, 2012, http://zootorah.com/essays/the-identity-of-the-nesher.

"They who wait ... wings like eagles."
Isaiah 40:31 RSV

"possessed no splendid form for us to see, no desirable appearance."
Isaiah 53:2

"A considerable ... into our right minds."
James Alison, lectures at House of Mercy, May 2005.

Olivia ... reading Bossypants *by Tina Fey.*
Tina Fey, *Bossypants* (New York: Reagan Arthur Books, 2011).

"Frowzy old saint ... do better?"
Margaret Atwood, *Selected Poems II: 1976–1986* (Boston: Houghton Mifflin, 1987), 75.

5. The Eagle—Power and Vulnerability
One bird named Alagym ... in one day.
I found this interesting detail and many others in Alice Parmelee's book *All the*

Birds of the Bible (New York: Harper, 1959). The story of Alagym is on page 119.

a pilot for the Buffalo Flying Service . . . five hundred eagles.
Dennis Drabelle, "Unfair Game," *Audubon Magazine,* accessed January 23, 2012, http://archive.audubonmagazine.org/archives/archives0801.html.

"a sense of smallness . . . ineradicably."
Erik Erikson, *Childhood and Society* (New York: Norton, 1993), 404.

"holding them in its claws mid-air . . . but as if it were rejecting a stranger."
I found this quotation in Graeme Gibson, *A Bedside Book of Birds* (New York: Doubleday, 2005), 323. He is quoting from *Peterborough Bestiary* MS 53 (early fourteenth century).

"taller than any of the people."
1 Samuel 9:2 RSV

"the whole world will know that there is a God on Israel's side."
1 Samuel 17:46

"Saul has killed his thousands, but David has killed his tens of thousands!"
1 Samuel 18:7

It sounds so much . . . in the very telling a veiled critique.
For a remarkable discussion of this, see Wes Howard-Brook's *"Come Out, My People": God's Call out of Empire in the Bible and Beyond* (Maryknoll, NY: Orbis, 2010).

"lest the land vomit you out when you defile it . . . before you."
Leviticus 18:28 RSV

"GOD was furious with Israel."
2 Kings 13:3 *THE MESSAGE*

"Whoever receives one such child . . . not me but him who sent me."
Mark 9:37 RSV

God doesn't come in power to save us . . . but in weakness.
I am very much indebted to Doug Frank's book *A Gentler God: Breaking Free of the Almighty in the Company of the Human Jesus* (Ann Arbor: Edward Brothers, 2010).

"Confession is the long slow process of being disarmed."
James Alison, lectures at House of Mercy, May 2005.

By 1963 there were only 417 nesting pairs . . . becoming weak.
For statistics on eagle populations, check out http://birds.audubon.org/species/baleag; www.eagles.org/vu-study/recovery/status.php; and many other sites on the Internet. It is difficult to estimate the current population exactly, but it is clear that it is burgeoning.

"Over increasingly large areas... are strangely silent."
Rachel Carson, *Silent Spring* (New York: Houghton Mifflin, 2002), 103.

6. The Ostrich—Comedy and Tragedy

"I have become like dust and ashes... a companion of ostriches."
Job 30:19, 29 RSV

"It is not his physical suffering or his personal losses... world in which he lived."
Abigail Pelham, *Contested Creations in the Book of Job: The-World-*as-*It-Ought-and-Ought-Not-to-Be* (Leiden: Brill, 2012), 61.

"After my speech... they couldn't believe it."
Job 29:22-24

"disdained... to set [them] with the dogs of [his] flock."
Job 30:1 RSV

"under the nettles... a senseless, a disreputable brood."
Job 30:7-8 RSV

We often feel so much sympathy for Job... privately obsessed with ourselves.
My reading of Job as an unreliable narrator comes from Abigail Pelham's discussion of "Job's Phantom Greatness" in *Contested Creations* (see above); and her discussion of Job as comedy in "Job as Comedy, Revisited," *Journal for the Study of the Old Testament* 35, no. 1 (2010).

"It is tragedy.... Comedy tells us the grandeur is a sham."
Pelham, "Job as Comedy," 110.

"God's questions direct Job's attention... diversely populated world."
Pelham, *Contested Creations,* 77.

"Tragedy admires man... sorry for him."
William Kerr, quoted in Pelham, "Job as Comedy," 94.

"It may be... the tragedy is that it is a comedy."
Pelham, "Job as Comedy," 93.

"Although we (usually) do not laugh at Job... in the least."
Pelham, "Job as Comedy," 95.

Frank Chapman... seven hundred women's hats he saw.
Paul Ehrlich, "Plume Trade," Stanford.edu, accessed February 13, 2012, www.stanford.edu/group/stanfordbirds/text/essays/Plume_Trade.html.

"imagine, when they have thrust their head... concealed."
Karl Kruszelnicki, "Ostrich Head in Sand," *Dr. Karl's Great Moments in Science* (ABC Science), accessed March 3, 2012, www.abc.net.au/science/articles/2006/11/02/1777947.htm.

"God has made her forget wisdom . . . understanding."
Job 39:17 RSV

Sidi Mohamed . . . protect them from rain.
For the story of Sidi Mohamed, see "True Stories of Real Mowglis and Other
Wild Children," Pustakmahal Publishers, accessed May 7, 2013, www.pustak
mahal.com/books/book.php/true-stories-real-mowglis-other-wild-children-
vikas-khatri/isbn-9788122313529/zb,,583,a,8,USD,a,a/index.html

Sometimes people read this poem . . . all God's greatness.
See Pelham, *Contested Creations,* esp. chap. 2, "Relationships Between Persons
in the World-as-It-Ought-and-Ought-Not-to-Be: Centrality and Dispersion,
Connectedness and Loneliness."

God satisfies "the waste and desolate land."
Job 38:27 RSV

"a world different from anything he could have conceived . . . madly loved."
Pelham, *Contested Creations,* 186.

"Whereas the world . . . 'Come out here and be free, as you were meant to be.'"
Ibid., 240–41.

"when she rouses herself to flee, she laughs at the horse and his rider."
Job 39:18 RSV

7. The Sparrow—Contempt and Compassion
"You are more important than the sparrow."
The actual translation in the RSV is "You are of more value than many spar-
rows" (Luke 12:7).

"Not one sparrow is forgotten in the sight of God."
The actual translation in the RSV is "not one of them is forgotten before God"
(Luke 12:6).

a Lutheran clergyman in Germany lobbied his local government . . . pesky beast.
Tim Birkhead, "The Wisdom of Birds," *Scientist,* accessed May 1, 2012,
www.the-scientist.com/?articles.view/articleNo/29569/title/Book-excerpt
-from-The-Wisdom-of-Birds/.

Two jawbones found in an ancient cave in Israel . . . at least occupies.
Rob Dunn "The Story of the Most Common Bird in the Word," *Smithsonian
Magazine,* accessed May 1, 2012, www.smithsonianmag.com/science
-nature/The-Story-of-the-Most-Common-Bird-in-the-World.html.

"Everyone come to fight sparrows."
Sha Yexin, "The Chinese Sparrow War of 1958," *EastSouthWestNorth* (August
31, 1997), accessed May 13, 2012, www.zonaeuropa.com/20061130_1.htm.

In their article . . . growing at the time.

Gary Alan Fine and Lazaros Christoforides, "Dirty Birds, Filthy Immigrants, and the English Sparrow War: Metaphorical Linkage in Constructing Social Problems," *Symbolic Interaction* 14, no. 4 (1991): 375–93.

"a foreigner that competes unfairly . . . eliminated from the American community of birds."
Ibid., 375.

"foreign vulgarians."
Ibid., 381.

"filthiness, sexual immorality . . . noisiness."
Ibid., 384.

"They increased very fast and spread . . . suffer the extreme penalty of the law."
Ibid., 386.

"all legislation protecting the sparrow . . . should be made illegal."
Ibid., 387.

One English newspaper offered a reward . . . peanuts in bird feeders.
Michael McCarthy, "Mystery of the Vanishing Sparrow," *Independent* (November 20, 2008), accessed May 20, 2012, www.independent.co.uk/ environment/nature/mystery-of-the-vanishing-sparrow-1026319.html.

A recent article in the UK's Daily Mail blames malaria . . . climate change.
Tamara Cohen, "Malaria Is Killing off Our Sparrows and Owls as Mosquitoes Invade," *Science and Tech* (August 15, 2011), accessed May 23, 2012, www .dailymail.co.uk/sciencetech/article-2025988/Malaria-killing-sparrows-owls -mosquitoes-invade.html.

An environmentalist . . . declared March 20, 2010, the first World Sparrow Day.
World Sparrow Day, accessed June 3, 2012, www.worldsparrowday.org /index.html.

"Sparrow Holi."
Indo-Asian News Service Rajeev, "This Year Celebrate Sparrow Holi," *WebINdia123* (March 20, 2011), accessed June 4, 2012, http://news.webindia 123.com/news/articles/India/20110320/1712631.html.

"On the eve of World Sparrow Day 2012 . . . 'seed to attract them.'"
"Save Sparrows for Nature's Balance," *Times of India* (March 21, 2012), accessed June 4, 2012, http://articles.timesofindia.indiatimes.com/2012-03-21/ kanpur/31219946_1_sparrows-and-other-birds-world-sparrow-day-bird-lover.

Apuleius, the ancient poet and philosopher . . . contempt.
"Apuleius Quotes," Quotations by Author, accessed June 20, 2012, www .quotationspage.com/quotes/Apuleius/.

"Every one who speaks a word against the Son of man . . . will not be forgiven."
Luke 12:10 RSV

In Australia they've learned to open automatic doors . . . the sensor.
Melinda LaBranche, "Sparrows That Open Doors," *Cornell Lab of Ornithology: All About Birds* (Winter 2004), accessed July 1, 2012, www.allaboutbirds.org/Page.aspx?pid=1261#top.

8. The Cock—Cockiness and Betrayal

"Avenger Farms offers fifteen different bloodlines . . . Owlsnest."
Avenger Farms, accessed December 18, 2012, http://avengerfarms .netau.net/bloodlines.htm.

"I owe a cock to Asclepios, Crito. Pay him without fail."
Phaedo, 115a. See Alan Dundes *The Cockfight: A Casebook* (Madison: University of Wisconsin Press, 1994), 192. This is a fascinating book that includes essays from authors in various disciplines, all writing about cockfighting.

One of the oldest representations of the fighting cock . . . sixth century BCE.
Jeffrey Zorn, "Tell en-Nasbeh: Biblical Mizpah" (adapted and expanded from "Nasbeh, Tell en-"), *The New Encyclopedia of Archaeological Excavations in the Holy Land,* ed. E. Stern, vol. 3 (Jerusalem: Carta, 1993), 1098–1102, accessed December 18, 2012, www.arts.cornell.edu/jrz3/frames2.htm.

Although cockfighting is illegal . . . it is a major national pastime.
Animal rights activists deplore it, but the lovers of the game insist that the fighting cock has a better life than most chickens these days. Factory-farmed chickens are debeaked at birth. They often never even see the great outdoors; and when it's time for slaughter they are hung upside down, stuck on a conveyor belt, and dunked in an electrically charged solution that is supposed to shock them to death, but doesn't always. Dead or alive, they then ride the belt to the kill room, where a knifelike instrument cuts their throats. Compared with such a life, cockfighters argue, their gamecocks live like kings. They are fed the best food, they are trained like athletes, and they get to run around outside every day. If they don't die in the ring, they are often retired after two or three fights to live out the rest of their lives in comparative luxury.

"crying like a chicken"
Dundes, *Cockfight,* 259.

"the mother's blood is showing"
Ibid., 211.

"As much of America surfaces in a ball park . . . that water runs downhill."
Ibid., 99.

"whatever goes into a man from outside can't defile him."
Mark 7:18 RSV

"Whoever wants to be first must be least of all and the servant of all."
Mark 9:35

"Whoever receives one such child . . . not me but him who sent me."
Mark 9:37 RSV

"This is my body, which is given for you."
Luke 22:19

"This cup is the new . . . poured out for you."
Luke 22:20

"For the Son of man . . . whom he is betrayed!"
Luke 22:22 RSV

"A dispute also arose among them, which of them was to be regarded as the greatest."
Luke 22:24 RSV

In a recent article in Harper's . . . age of man.
David Samuels, "Wild Things: Animal Nature, Human Racism, and the Future of Zoos," *Harper's* 324, no. 1945 (June 2012): 28–42.

An eminent biologist who helped to eradicate smallpox . . . next hundred years.
Nawal Mahmood, "Eminent Scientist Claims Humans Will Be Extinct in 100 Years," *Tech Journal* (June 28, 2010), accessed December 18, 2012, http://thetechjournal.com/science/eminent-scientist-claims-humans-will-be-extinct-in-100-years.xhtml.

"The more that scientists look at the way the world operates . . . If the universe were not more cooperative than it is competitive, it would fall apart."
Colin Tudge, *The Bird: A Natural History of Who Birds Are, Where They Came From, and How They Live* (New York: Random House, 2008), 427.

there is no redemption without brokenness.
I depend on James Alison's reading of Peter in *Raising Abel: The Recovery of the Eschatological Imagination* (New York: Crossroad, 2003), 88–94.

"Even though they all fall away, I will not."
Mark 14:29 RSV

"Truly, I say to you, this very night . . . you will deny me three times."
Mark 14:30 RSV

"If I must die with you, I will not deny you."
Mark 14:31 RSV

"remembered how Jesus had said . . . And [Peter] broke down and wept."
Mark 14:72 RSV

Maybe because our understanding . . . kingdoms of the world.
I depend, again, deeply on James Alison for his discussion of the self formed in rivalry and competition rather than in mutuality and love and the need for this self to be broken open. This theme appears in many of his books. See *Undergoing God: Dispatches from the Scene of a Break-In* (New York:

Bloomsbury, 2006); *On Being Liked* (New York: Crossroad, 2004); and Alison, *Raising Abel.*

9. The Hen—Freedom and Domestication
"O Jerusalem, Jerusalem, killing the prophets...as a hen gathers her brood under her wings, and you would not!"
Matthew 23:37 RSV

"arose that detestable gourmandise and gluttonie...which creatures Nature had allowed the wide aire for their scope and habitation."
Pliny the Elder, *Natural History,* 23–79. Quoted in Graeme Gibson, *A Bedside Book of Birds* (New York: Doubleday, 2005) 257.

"I'd like to focus on the resurrection.... Grace still exists even if the darkness covers it."
Sonja Olson, sermon delivered at House of Mercy, Passion Sunday, 2012.

Think of Warner Sallman's Head of Christ.
For the following information about Warner Sallman, see David Morgan, ed., *Icons of American Protestantism: The Art of Warner Sallman* (New Haven, CT: Yale University Press, 1996).

"whoever gives to one of these little ones even a cup of cold water."
Matthew 10:42 RSV

I'm not sure how we could trust or love an almighty God...a better world.
Doug Frank, in *A Gentler God: Breaking Free of the Almighty in the Company of the Human Jesus* (Ann Arbor: Edward Brothers, 2010), speaks of this more articulately than I am able. I've been very influenced by his work in this book (and beyond).

"If Christ is weak and humble on earth, then God is weak and humble in heaven."
Jürgen Moltmann, *The Trinity and the Kingdom: The Doctrine of God,* quoted in Frank, *Gentler God,* 185.

"Do you also want to leave?"
John 6:67

What Luther saw...the only god that can help us.
See Elie Wiesel writing about the Holocaust in *Night* (New York: Farrar, Straus and Giroux, 2006).

"God simply does not have the kind of power we ourselves crave."
Frank, *Gentler God,* 208.

10. The Raven—Failure and Trust
"Look at the birds in the sky."
Matthew 6:26

"Consider the ravens."
Luke 12:24

In the book of Proverbs, we meet ravens... disobedient children.
See Proverbs 30:17.

In the prophetic writings of Isaiah... and the jackals.
See Isaiah 34.

In some ancient... failed to return to the ark.
John F. Adams, "Classical Raven Lore and Poe's Raven," in *Poe Studies* 5, no. 2 (December 1972).

Early Christian commentators frequently comment... failed Noah.
See David Marcus, "The Mission of the Raven (Gen. 8:7)," paper presented at the Jewish Theological Seminary of America, available at www.jtsa.edu/documents/pagedocs/janes/2002%2029/marcus29.pdf.

"arrogant and shamelessly impudent... might have led to folly."
Ralph Marcus, *Philo: Questions and Answers on Genesis* (Cambridge, MA: Harvard University Press, 1963), 114.

"procrastinators."
Jack P. Lewis, *A Study of the Interpretation of Noah and the Flood in Jewish and Christian Literature* (Leiden: Brill, 1968), 174.

"How great is your faith!"
Actual CEB translation is "Woman, you have great faith" (Matthew 15:28).

"there were three that engaged... the dog."
Talmud, Sanhedrin 108b.

"The wolf seems... pleasure in the company of ravens."
Barry Lopez, *Of Wolves and Men* (New York: Scribner, 1978), 67.

Bernd Heinrich... men playing guitars.
Bernd Heinrich, *The Mind of the Raven: Investigations and Adventures with Wolf-Birds* (New York: Harper Collins, 1999), 46.

"the raven retorts to Noah with a winning argument."
BT Sanhedrin 108b.

"Should the Master of heat or the Master of cold attack me... type of creature?"
BT Sanhedrin 108b.

Other rabbis suggest... had designs on its mate.
BT Sanhedrin 108b; Rashi at Genesis 8:7.

One theory purports that it is unclean because of its morose and solitary lifestyle.
I found this interpretation at www.powershow.com/view1/168110-M2I2Z/Laws_Concerning_Clean_and_Unclean_Food_powerpoint_ppt_ presentation (accessed Dec 20, 2012).

"and the ravens brought him... and meat in the evening."
1 Kings 17:6 RSV

ABOUT THE AUTHOR

Debbie Blue (MA, Yale Divinity School) is one of the founding pastors of House of Mercy, a church in St. Paul, Minnesota. She is the author of *Sensual Orthodoxy* and *From Stone to Living Word*. Reverend Blue's sermon podcasts are listened to by subscribers around the world, and her essays, sermons, and reflections on the scripture have appeared in a wide variety of publications including *Life in Body, Proclaiming the Scandal of the Cross, Geez, The Image Journal,* and *The Christian Century*. Debbie and her family live with friends on a farm near Milaca, Minnesota.